Contents

CU00729488

Acknowledgments

Writing this book has been a long journey. It started with my parents' decision to move to Scotland from Africa and culminated in the completion of this book. Without my parents' decision to move to the UK, I would not be who I am today. I am grateful to Christ for this opportunity! My family, friends and countless acquaintances have been a large pool of inspiration and encouragement. I hope this book encourages you all. Please, enjoy the experience!

For Africa... For Scotland... For Afro-Scots.

STORY BY MICHAEL JONATHAN
DITED BY LAURA KENZIE WILLIAMS

Introduction

The book features the infusion of African & Scottish culture. This is the theme which distinguishes Afro-Scot from other brands. UZOR hopes to share his own & others experiences as an African growing up in Scotland to demonstrate how conflicting cultural assimilation can be. These three stories ('A-FROSCOT', 'What Is Nka?', and 'The Afro-Scot Experience') demonstrate how cross-cultural influences can fire up creativity. They explore how diversity leads to creativity. The author desires to give the reader the opportunity to piece all three stories together to understand what 'The Afro-Scot Experience' is. This particular narrative tells the story of an African-Glaswegian high-school student who struggles with his identity. He hopes to find it through surrounding himself with people who are African, but this only deepens his insecurity. How will he break the cultural barrier that many Africans have struggled with?

You could cut the tension with a knife. A group of African and White Scottish boys square up to each other. Uzor felt like he was underwater, too deep to grasp oxygen. Suddenly, A flurry of fists are exchanged, and the scene becomes gruesome. It immediately escalates, men with police badges come racing out of their Vauxhall. Uzor couldn't think clearly... How did I get to this?!

Chapter 1

Childhood

Walking up the road during lunchtime at St. Scot Secondary School with his White Scottish friends, Uzor begins to feel the common feeling of exclusion and lone liness as his 'friends' begin teasing him for his brown chocolate skin that his ancestors wore proudly. Uzor tries holding in his tears. Another, amongst many victims of Scottish racism, who choose to hide their misery instead of confront it. Racism was rampant in Glasgow at this time, since Glasgow had yet to diversify in the way that other cities in the UK had, the ethnic majority was staggeringly white, British. It was rare to see another African person walking down the street, let alone living in the area in which Uzor was raised. This made someone like Uzor seem rather alien to a large percentage of Scottish people, who hadn't ventured far from their comfort zones, and in many cases, far from Glasgow. Everything about Uzor's appearance was new to them, from the curly hair, the round wide nose, wrinkly fingers and big lips. To them he was a new species.

Uzor's friends turn into the school gates but Uzor walks on further.

'Where are you going?' shouted Steven. One of Uzor's so-called Scottish 'friends', scuttling towards Uzor with an arrogant, mocking, demeanor. Steven cracks a devious smile as he checks Uzor's face. When he sees that Uzor is fighting back tears, he just laughs at him harder. Uzor pulls his hoodie down to cover his face. He then walks all the way home and locks himself in his room.

Growing up Uzor didn't know who he was. His mother and father were both from Africa, but moved to Glasgow when he was three years of age. He spent most of his childhood playing video games like other Scottish children trying desperately hard to fit in.

Uzor heard his mother's voice coming up the stairs.

'Uzor, head back to school right now!' She shouted as her feet smacked each step, making their way up to his bedroom.

His mother was a disciplinarian and didn't value laziness. As a result, Uzor had to reluctantly get up, leave his bedroom, and head back to school.

He checked his Nokia and saw anxiously that he was now late for class. He sadly walked up the stairs to his classroom. He reached the third floor and lowered his head as he pressed the door handle to his maths class.

'Why are you late?' said the teacher, before Uzor was even half-way through the door.

'I was at the toilet.' Said Uzor, as he took his seat. Everybody in the class was staring at him. It was as if they all knew. Throughout the corner of his eyes, Uzor noticed Steven's smug face. Embarrassed by the situation and upset that he'd allow his friends to make him feel so ashamed, Uzor started to contemplate if these were the people he should be surrounding himself with.

Growing up in a Scottish environment, not a day would go by without someone marking Uzor out as different because of his skin colour. Uzor had a knack for lying to his Scottish friends about his 'black friends' outside of school in order to look more cool and more 'black'.

He thought, If I want to fit in, I must behave like a black stereotype. So, he proceeded to spend the majority of his childhood life playing up to traditional black stereotypes. It didn't help that every day he was faced with racist remarks: comments about his skin colour, and questions or comments about where he was 'from'. He slowly began to integrate himself into the Scottish culture, learning slang and adopting the Glaswegian accent until he sounded like a Ned (A Non Educated Delinquent). However, even despite his unwavering efforts, Uzor never felt truly accepted and welcomed by his Scottish 'friends'. Although he avoided the terrible treatment that other Africans who couldn't talk in a Scottish accent faced, he was still plagued with racist comments on a daily basis.

'Shut up Uzor you are a nigga!'

We Provide Delivery in Nigeria & Ghana

Subscription errand services for Buying groceries or setting up grocery with pocket money plan for loved ones anywhere in Nigeria & Ghana

What We Offer

Pocket Money
Using pocket money, change your currency and transfer money to friends and families in Nigeria and Ghana

Grocery
Order products that would be purchased and delivered to friends and families in Nigeria and Ghana

Special offers
With special offer package, get to know about the latest discounts and promo options

How do we do it?

01 Your subscription plan is received

02 The items are received and sorted out

03 At the scheduled time, it gets delivered

04 You receive a notification on the success of delivery and confirmation from the recipient.

BlissSub
SUBSCRIPTION SERVICES

GET IT ON Google Play

Download on the App Store

♪ f 🖸 🐦 @BlissSub

Was a sentence he heard often. Comments like this would always end-up with both sides (the people who said t, and Uzor) having sore faces and a school suspension. It eventually reached a point that racist, verbal abuse was something Uzor just had to laugh off. The fighting wasn't worth the repeated broken noses.

He decided to seek change, when one of his aunties (who wasn't in fact a blood relative, but a close friend of his mother) whom Uzor hadn't seen in a while came to visit. Uzor greeted her fondly. He quickly remembered that this auntie's son, Jack, was his childhood friend from primary school. He thought that reconnecting with Jack might be a good way to surround himself with black friends, who would make his life better.
We are brothers!'

This is what Uzor always heard black activists say, but Uzor was painfully aware that he had few black brothers...
...He decided it was time to find his brothers.
As if his aunty could read Uzor's mind, she said, 'You guys should meet! It's been so long!'
So, they set up a date and time for Uzor to go to Jack's house. This boosted Uzor's morale as he thought Jack could be his ticket to a better life... Well, he naively thought. Travelling in his aunt's car to her house to meet Jack, Uzor felt excitement welling up inside of him. He put his earphones in, playing jazz music.

He looked out to the motorway to take in the beauty of sunny Glasgow. They arrived at the house and as Uzor enters he notices that Jack isn't in. He walks towards the kitchen to see a young primary-school aged girl. She was Jack's sister.

'Hi Lisa, how are you?' said Uzor.

'Jack left to the shops and is coming back soon,' said Lisa with a stern face. She had quite the attitude.

Taken aback by Lisa's response, Uzor composed himself. 'Thank you," he said before walking into the living room to wait for Jack.

He sat close to the window and looked through the blinds, eagerly anticipating Jacks return. The living room was dark and didn't look that different from when he was last at their house many years ago. The only thing that moved was the tv, closer to the middle of the room. African's aren't notorious for having incredibly done up houses. We were very straight forward people.

Uzor became bored of observing the home and flicked up his Nokia to start playing Snake, when at the side of his eye, through the blinds he saw Jack at the main door. He entered the house and walked into the living room to see Uzor.

'Yoooo!' Said Jack, as they both hugged each other.

'How have you been, man?' said Uzor.

'Living life' Jack replied, as he led Uzor upstairs, where, to Uzor's surprise they entered the toilet.

'Why are we here?' said Uzor.

'Do you smoke?' asked Jack.

To which Uzor replied, 'No'.

They both went downstairs and headed towards the backyard, where Jack knew he couldn't be seen by his mother. He sparked the blunt and started smoking as Uzor watched in surprise, observing the differences in Jack. The way he dressed, his demeanor... so much had changed. Jack was now more like a gang member than the childhood friend Uzor remembered. Uzor's naïve optimism that had manifested in the car journey to Jacks house was shattered. The air smelt like a greenhouse, or like walking into a catholic church after incense has been burnt . However, one thing that didn't change was Jack's natural charisma. He just had a presence about him.

'Uzor!' Jacked exclaimed excitedly, clearly high from the cannabis, snapping Uzor out of his daydream, 'What you saying?' said Jack, trying to get a conversation going.

Uzor wasn't a smoker, so he held his breath from time to time to avoid inhaling cancer, but tried to not show discomfort, making an effort for Jack not to notice. Jack and Uzor then went around the area catching up with each other. After a few hours they arrived at a bus stop. The unusual Scottish heat was biting at their skin as they said their goodbyes.

'Today was calm still!' Said Jack. 'I'll be out in town tomorrow. Let me know if you aren't too busy bro'.

Uzor got on the incoming Bus 61 back to town.

The trip around the area had put a smokescreen around the dangerous influence of Jack, but even so, Uzor wanted a new lifestyle where he was surrounded by black people. He resolved to meet Jack in town on Saturday. He still wanted to fit in somewhere – a relatable and common sentiment to all black kids growing up in Scotland.

Chapter 2

African Friends

The next day, standing inside the crowded bus, Uzor held the turquoise handles to balance. The bus stopped in town and Uzor thanked the driver. It was a common thing for bus drivers to be appreciated in Glasgow. Uzor got off the bus and immediately found it difficult to walk in a straight line because of how crowded the city was. Uzor wore navy shorts, a thin white t-shirt and bright shoes to match the weather. The bold pigeons covered the street while the artists, buskers, and homeless took their places at the side of the streets. There was a thick smell of cigarette smoke and mould that tickled his nostrils. A normal day in Glasgow City Centre. Uzor crossed the road at St Enoch to walk up Buchanan street, possibly the busiest street on a Saturday afternoon. The key to maneuvering was to be as quick as possible. When Uzor reached the steps at Buchanan Galleries he saw Jack by himself smoking a cigarette. Jack noticed Uzor and made his way down the stairs to dap him up. The handshake was awkward as Uzor wasn't used to that type of greeting.

He tried to ease the tension with an awkward laugh. He noticed that there was something odd about the way Jack was dressed today. He was wearing a black fleece and track bottoms. Very strange for a hot summer's day. However, Uzor chose to ignore this.

'What's the plans today?' said Uzor nervously. Jack took one more puff of his cigarette before throwing it on the ground.

'This way!' said Jack, as they both started to descend Buchanan street towards St Enoch. 'I have to meet the boys for some plans.'

It was a rather ambiguous answer but Uzor shook away the negative thoughts and went along. As they walked, Uzor noticed that Jack knew everybody. They would constantly have to stop to have a chat with his acquaintances. It was as if Jack was a gang leader, or just a charismatic person that everybody happened to know. This made Jack seem even more mysterious. They ended up at the Four Corners and walked into KFC. At KFC, Uzor was surprised to see so many Africans and Asians in once space. They were all talking and laughing. They nearly filled up the whole ground floor. As soon as Jack appeared before them they all stopped what they were doing and approached him to dap him up. Jack walked around talking to everybody while Uzor followed. Jack introduced Uzor to everyone. This made everyone warm to him and made Uzor feel less anxious. Uzor admired how Jack made socializing look so easy.

'You know, all of the girls like you!' said Alicia. Uzor's face grew warm as he blushed. He looked to the side to see one of the girls staring at him seductively. He quickly looked away, showing his inexperience with the opposite sex. Suddenly, Jack grabbed his attention.

'We are heading to the shops... Coming?'

Uzor nodded at Jack and followed him as he walked alongside Pride & Alicia. They head towards the convenience store to 'buy' some snacks.

Before they entered the store, Uzor noticed many people wearing Celtic scarfs, it was a match day. Pride accidentally bumped into one and they retaliate verbally.

'Ya black bastard!'

The Celtic supporter's abuse didn't even register to Uzor, until a couple seconds after he had entered the store. Uzor looked back slightly to see Pride poke his head out of the convenience store and shout angrily at the men after they had passed the store

'Shut the fuck up!' The Celtic supporter and his mate turned & walked aggressively towards the convenience store. Pride ran to the back of the store, clearly anxious, but filled with adrenaline. The men, clearly drunk, approach Pride in the store.

Pride shouted, 'Jack, Yo Jack!'

Jack composed himself while looking at the men. Pride, not wanting to look weak, tried to confront the men, but fell back as they aimed their Buckfast bottles at Pride's head.

Uzor stayed motionless at the back of the shop. His mind racing fast. The experience at the store was like the phenomenon when time slows down before an accident. He was surprisingly composed. He was trying to think of how to escape. Pride was hot headed and didn't think things through. How do we escape? Uzor thought, as his back made contact with the Cola bottle rack at the back of the store, making a noise. A different Celtic supporter turned and looked at him with malevolent eyes, putting his hand inside his shorts. Uzor wasn't sure if he was bluffing, but he didn't want to find out whether or not he actually held a knife. The shopkeeper, equally anxious, rang an alarm bell, signaling a call to the police. The Celtic supporters quickly escaped, and the group of perplexed Black-Glaswegian's left the shop a few seconds later. After that encounter, Uzor couldn't stop looking behind his shoulders, worrying that the Celtic supporters would come back for revenge. Jack, Pride and Alicia walked on ahead as if nothing had happened. It was as if this was a normal day for them. This terrified Uzor.

These guys are crazy! Uzor thought.

They crossed the road towards Central Station and Uzor told them he'd forgotten something back at KFC. This was an obvious lie, but Uzor did it to avoid another terrifying encounter with the Celtic fans. Walking back, one of the girls who was eyeing him up earlier approached Uzor and started flirting. As they were talking, Uzor noticed Jack sprinting with Pride and Alicia.

Uzor decided to follow them, leaving the girl behind as he sprinted after them. They ended up at an underground car park.

'I saw you guys running! what's up!?' panted Uzor.

Jack started rolling a joint, 'We stole this weed' he laughed. He lit the joint and they started passing it around. Jack offered some to Uzor, but Uzor politely declined. Uzor felt his stomach turn at how calm they were. They all talked in a lingo he couldn't understand, but still, to fit in, Uzor shook his head and smiled.

Deep down he knew the situation he was in, and reality began to dawn on him. This isn't what I expected! He thought... he thought right!

A Vauxhall slowly rolled into the car park, and the vibe suddenly changed. Behind him Uzor heard men with Glasgwegian accents angrily stomping into the car park. Jack was the first to notice and let the group know by exclaiming.

'There's no way I'm running! We will deal with them here!'

Uzor now found himself in a far worse situation than he had ever been in with his Scottish friends. The men who approached them all wore different coloured tracksuits with Nike caps and Nike TNS. What shocked him most was that one of them was his friend Steven. Steven was too blinded by rage to notice Uzor.

'Geez our fucking weed' said one of them angrily.

Uzor's stomach lurched as one of them pulled out a lockback knife.

'Fuck off!' said Jack assertively.

This escalated the situation and a fight broke out. The knife gets knocked out of the man's hands and the fight turns into a bloody mess of fists and feet on skin and bone. The fight soon stops as two undercover policemen jump out of their Vauxhall. They all scatter. Pride & Alicia manage to get away, but Uzor was at the very back avoiding the fight so he didn't notice a rock behind him and as he turned to run, he fell. The two policemen handcuff Jack, Steven & Uzor. Uzor struggled but the cuffs were too tight. Uzor thought he was in a movie and was struggling to face reality.

The three boys were split up into three different police cars, so Uzor's contact with Jack and Steven was cut off. The drive to the police station felt like an eternity. Finally, Uzor's car reached the police station. The police started interrogating him and Uzor started acting like a deranged character in a detective movie. Deep down Uzor was doing this as a way to avoid accepting the reality of the situation. The room Uzor was in was all painted blue and smelt like cement. He was still handcuffed. The Police managed to find Uzor's identity and decided that Uzor wasn't part of the case.

'You are one lucky man!' Said the chief policeman. 'You aren't one of the men involved in this drug case.'

'Drug case! What have I gotten myself into?!' Uzor thought as he tried to stop his legs from shaking.

Due to Uzor being too young to leave at any time they kept him overnight in a small red painted cell. The only thing that kept him company was the hard, blue mat, the dirty toilet at the side of the room, a small window on the ceiling and the biting cold. So many thoughts raced through his head. 'Should I escape through that window? Should I crack through the walls?' thought Uzor as the movie Shawshank Redemption played through his mind. However, after a few minutes, reality dawned on him. It struck him like a thunderbolt and Uzor burst into tears.

'How long will I be here for?' Uzor shouted, as his chest tightened up from anxiety. One of the security guards heard Uzors cry and responded mockingly.

'Could be a week or two.'

The security guard only said that knowing how innocent and gullible Uzor was. Uzor had reached the lowest point. This is what he got for trying to fit in. Uzor was led out of his cell and had his photo taken to be put in a record.

'How will your parents react?' said one of the staff.

Uzor didn't respond. Now back in his cell, Uzor forced himself to sleep. An activity depressed individuals participate in to avoid intense mental anguish. The constant loud banging of the cell doors and wailing from the other inmates made it even harder to sleep.

A few hours later, although it felt like several days, Uzor woke up to the sound of the security guard offering him breakfast. The breakfast consisted of a Frosties breakfast bar and a mug filled with hot chocolate. Uzor ate the bar but avoided the hot chocolate. 'It could be contaminated', thought Uzor. The security guard once again called his name.

'Your mother is here to pick you up.'

... It was a rather quiet journey home.

Chapter 3

The African Party

Uzor received a letter through the door telling him that he had been assigned as a witness to the drugs case. A few days later, Uzor headed out to buy some hair products in the city centre. While walking up Buchanan street Uzor noticed a tall, light skin man wearing a black blazer that matched his trousers and derby shoes. He walked with an air of confidence, holding a very expensive leather duffle bag. He was walking into ZARA with determined speed. It was obvious he was a man who valued his time. Something about the man struck Uzor. It was as if Uzor had known him in a past life. Uzor followed him into the store. Inside the marble-floored interior of ZARA, Uzor saw the man walking downstairs into the men's section. Uzor maneuvered around the many mannequins and tables of clothing and lightly jogged downstairs to see the man checking out a puffer jacket. Suddenly it struck him that he knew this man. It was Sammy, his childhood friend.

Uzor remembered him from back in the days when Sammy's mother and his were very close friends before Sammy and his family moved away to live in Angola. Uzor approached him.

'Sammy! Whats good bro?'.
Sammy turned around to see who called him and for a split second looked confused. He realised who it is, and, in excitement hugged Uzor.

'Bro, how have you been? You look great!' said Sammy.

'Can say the same for you!' Uzor said as he looked at Sammy with admiration.

You see Sammy was similar to Uzor. He grew up in a bad neighborhood and still had both parents in the house. However, his father was Italian and his mother was Angolan. He grew up in Glasgow rather unaware of who he was. Was he Italian, Angolan or was he Scottish? Was he black or white? Uzor and Sammy would regularly meet up to talk about characters in cartoons and Uzor would notice a slight difference in how Sammy talked to him and others. To Uzor, he would retain the African accent and would freely use pidgin slang. However, to other Glaswegians he would adopt a thick Glasgwegian accent, whilst, to his father he would speak in an Italian accent.

He always thought he had to fit in, but now as Uzor looked at him in the present he knew something was very different.

Aside from his immaculate dressing, Sammy had a glimmer in his eye, and talked with an accent you couldn't put your finger on. It was as if Sammy had mixed all the identities he used to switch between into one. He was self-aware. Uzor admired him but also envied what he had. 'How could I get this for myself?' Uzor wondered. Sensing Uzor's insecurities, Sammy handed Uzor a small poster-card from his duffle bag.

'My girlfriend is hosting an African party this weekend, we can catch up proper there.'

Uzor took the card and headed home, mentally preparing his outfits as he went. Uzor wanted to peer into Sammy's world and hopefully grab the self-assertion and confidence that Sammy had for himself.

It was now the weekend and Uzor was late to the event. Uzor's taxi stopped in front of the venue and he was immediately surprised at the amount of people in attendance. They were outside talking and taking pictures. Uzor walked inside the building towards a long corridor. He struggled to walk in between the crowds of people. Uzor finally walked through and nearly tripped as children ran past him in their game of tig. He walked into the main hall and the sheer amount of people inside overwhelmed him. They all wore their African garments from their countries. The Congolese men wore their bright jeweled yellow and green suits and the Nigerian men wore their dashikis and native trousers.

The women wore their Ankara dresses. Uzor looked to the side of the hall to see a huge line of people waiting to get served some rice, pounded yam and soups. The food list was endless.

'Uzor!' shouted Sammy.

Sammy approached Uzor wearing a black native shirt and trousers. It contrasted with Uzor's white native wear. However, Uzor still felt underdressed. Everyone just looked lovely. Following Sammy was his girlfriend. She wore tight braids and a lovely Ankara dress.

'Nice to meet you' she said as Sammy introduced her to Uzor. Uzor chatted with Sammy a bit before he left. Just like Jack, Sammy also had the It-factor but Sammy was a classy man. He gracefully walked around the room, effortlessly greeting people and putting them at ease. Uzor sat in the corner of the room and observed the party. An afrobeat song began to play and, like clockwork, everyone emerged onto the dancefloor. Uzor watched in awe, mainly because Uzor hadn't ever really taken the time to sit and observe the African culture before. Of course, this wasn't the first time Uzor had been to an African party, but this was the first time he had experienced one. Sammy grabbed Uzor's hand to dance and Uzor reluctantly got up from his seat. Soon enough, Uzor was shaking around the dancefloor. The energy was too hard to resist.

Eventually, tired of dancing, Sammy and Uzor went to grab food. The line had settled as everyone stayed at the front to dance.

There were two empty seats at the eating area.
Although Uzor had eaten jollof before, Uzor had never
stopped and appreciated it as a dish that was such an
integral part of his identity. Uzor thankfully ate the
food. Sammy noticed, and with a roaring laughter said
'Man's hungry!'.

Uzor nearly choked with laughter.

Uzor waited for the food to digest before he went
back into the dancefloor. Sammy immediately got up,
and before heading to the front mentioned to Uzor that
he would be going on a trip around Scotland next week
for a photography project and invited Uzor to join him.
Uzor gratefully, and excitedly accepted the invitation.

The day to leave for the trip came around quickly.
Uzor hopped into Sammy's car and they immediately
headed for Glencoe, their first destination.

Chapter 4

Tour Around Scotland

They took the Kingston bridge heading towards the A82 that took them straight to Loch Lomond and then Glencoe. Uzor rolled the windows down to inhale the Scottish air. He marveled at the sights around him as he witnessed the copper coloured sun-rays shine off the trees, buildings and far away mountains. Uzor started to play music through the car Bluetooth and they both relaxed to some smooth jazz.

'Have you been this far up Scotland?' asked Sammy.

Uzor pondered on the question. He knew he had travelled around Scotland with his family before, but like the African parties and food, he hadn't taken the time to appreciate the view and indulge in the moment, never fully experiencing Scotland's beauty.

'This is my first time traveling' said Uzor.

Uzor only said it was his first time because Uzor wanted to experience it like it was his first time. This allowed him to remove any expectations and relax. As they drove over the Erskine bridge, Uzor looked to his left to see the ant-like buildings below. It was like they were in the sky above everyone. 'So this is what it means to fly,' Uzor thought to himself. Uzor was experiencing everything like a newborn child. They were twisting and turning. Sammy grabbed his attention by pointing to the wide loch at his right. Uzor was taken aback by the pebbles of light which seemed to skip along the lake. Photographs just didn't do it justice. It was something only a present human being could experience. They passed through the green painted bridges and the small streams of water descending from the rocks before they finally entered Glencoe. Immediately, the presence of the mountains consumed Uzor as he stared at them in awe. They made him feel incredibly small. Far away to his left, was a snowy mountain, it was like it had its own separate seasons. To his right were mountains so close Uzor felt he could hug them. In front of him was a long road which stretched for miles... An endless adventure.

'Look at that!' said Sammy, who pointed to a small house sitting at the foot of a mountain. The house seemed so close, but it stretched for several miles, swamped by the vast mountain behind it. The interesting thing was that even though it was small it still stood out. Uzor felt a strange connection to the little white cottage.

To others it might look insignificant, because it may seem like a miniscule human detail amongst the overwhelming natural sea of mountains that surrounded it. However, it accepted its place and stood out powerfully because of it. They parked not too far away from the mountains to see the house properly. Sammy stepped out to take some photographs while Uzor walked around the terrain. Uzor couldn't walk too far in fear of falling into a mud pit. He looked around and started to feel an overwhelming sense of freedom. Uzor didn't realise how beautiful Scotland was. Uzor spent most of his childhood not really aware of how beautiful things were. He felt like he had spent so much of his time wanting to be anywhere but where he was, he had forgotten to enjoy the exciting opportunities and experiences of the country and city he was raised in. He thought that perhaps this was true of all people.

On the car ride back home, feeling restless, they stopped at a service station for a toilet break. Sammy went to the toilet leaving Uzor to curiously walk around. The station had a cafe that served regular rolls and sandwiches. Inside the cafe was a 1950s interior with bright red chairs that mixed well with the pink ceiling, cocaine white floors and bright, blinding lights. Something caught Uzor's attention near the counter. A statue of a man sporting an afro, a kilt and bagpipes.

'Do my eyes deceive me' Uzor thought to himself.

Uzor looked again properly and realised it wasn't an afro but a feather bonnet. Uzor laughed out loud, allowing Sammy to find him.

'Why are you laughing?' asked Sammy. Uzor pointed towards the statue explaining how he had misconceived the feather bonnet for an afro. They both started laughing. Suddenly, an idea hit Uzor who started to give thought to the possibility of fusing two contrasting cultures together...

What would happen if African and Scottish culture came together? What could we create?

Uzor kept this idea to himself as they left the cafe with some sandwiches and rolls. They headed back on the road back to Glasgow. Uzor struggled with this idea for hours. It was as if everything he was seeing was forcing him to accept who he was and this statue was the most blatant example. Uzor started to grow restless and in frustration asked Sammy a very peculiar question that startled him.

'How did you come to accept yourself?'.

Without judging, or asking Uzor why he was asked, Sammy rested in his chair, raising his thinking face to a beaming smile and said with a slightly discernible breath 'I realised that I was a very rare person. Out of all the African people who could be brought here, I was one of them and I wouldn't trade myself for anyone else.'.

It was like thunder had struck Uzor!

Chapter 5

The Court Case

Several weeks later, the day of the court case had arrived. Uzor anxiously shut his umbrella and placed it under his armpit as he entered the court building. Uzor quickly looked at the nearby window to check his reflection, double checking his black suit for any stains he might have missed. 'At least I look good', he thought, quietly enjoying his new-found confidence in who he was.

Uzor walked to the counter to get his details taken. One of the bodyguards at the side of the building approached him to take him upstairs. Whilst inside the see-through glass-bottomed lift, Uzor started to notice things about Glasgow he'd never paid attention to before. Like the juxtaposition between the old buildings and the modern buildings and how a person hardly looks up because of the lack of tall buildings in the city. The odd occasion you did look up you would marvel at the intricate architecture.

WHO ARE YOU?! WHO ARE YOU?! WHO ARE YOU?!

Uzor looked around the courtroom to see everybody's eyes upon him as the judge asked him to explain what happened on the day of the stolen drugs. His mouth dried up.

'Do you swear to tell the truth, the whole truth and nothing but the truth' said the Courtroom Judge.

It was as if Uzor was being forced to pick a side. What would Uzor do?

'Mr.Uzor, I want you to explain what happened on the day of the arrest,' said the Judge.

Uzor raises his head to see the Judge. Jack and Steven's eyes pierced through his body and into his soul. His voice trembled as he tried to speak. WHO ARE YOU?! WHO ARE YOU?! WHO ARE YOU?! Still bellowing in his head, increasing in volume, until it felt like someone was screaming directly into his ear. He nearly choked. However, the memory of the African party, the small house at Glencoe, the statue, and the various beautiful landscapes Uzor saw with Sammy immediately flashed through his mind. Uzor had to make a decision. Finally, he stood straight, took a deep breath, and with a confident voice declared

'I am an AfroScot!'

This confused the courtroom. Everyone looked at Uzor, but he felt incredibly elated. A natural high.

His powerful demeanor and assertive eyes were not of a nervous boy, but that of a self-assured man. Jack and Steven looked at him startled. It was as though this new, self-confident Uzor was an entirely different person.

Hours later, the court hearing having ended, Uzor sought a place to sit and breathe for a moment. He chose the spot next to the vending machine, where he'd sat anxiously before the hearing. He reminisced about Sammy's answer to his question on their way back to Glasgow those few weeks ago and how much that one answer had altered his perspective on life. As he looked out the window, everything about Glasgow was vibrant: the trees, the brown buildings, the sky, and people. Uzor immediately took out his notebook and started jotting down an idea for an event he wanted to create. 'AfroScot', a party fusing both Scottish and African cultures together, where the dress code was simply a mixture of both traditional wears. It was a way for him to show the world his triumph and to help others like him to realise their own identities.

Chapter 6

Resolution

A few months later Uzor held the event at the same hall as the African party he had met Sammy and his girlfriend at. Sammy helped him out with the decoration and last-minute prep before the opening. He was nervous & uncertain of how the event would go, but still proud regardless of what he had already accomplished. The doors opened and a crowd of people rushed into the event dressed elaborately. The men wore their kilts and native African shirts with shoes to match, whilst the women wore their own kilts with hems that touched their shins alongside African jewelry, to match the dress code. The food being served was a mixture of various African foods, followed by Scottish desserts, like shortbread and tablet. It was fun seeing haggis being eaten with jollof rice. The night was a great success, with everyone of different colours and ethnic backgrounds partying together.

Everything came full circle and Uzor was so overwhelmed by his own journey that he wept. He had finally come to terms with himself and the wonderful serenity of peace now resided within him.

A short while after the party, Uzor came home to the news that the 'AfroScot' event had grabbed the attention of local MPs and they wanted to fund another event. Uzor jumped up, unable to contain his joy when he heard the news. Now he had found his purpose. To help others understand who they are and learn to accept it.

Accept and love yourself.

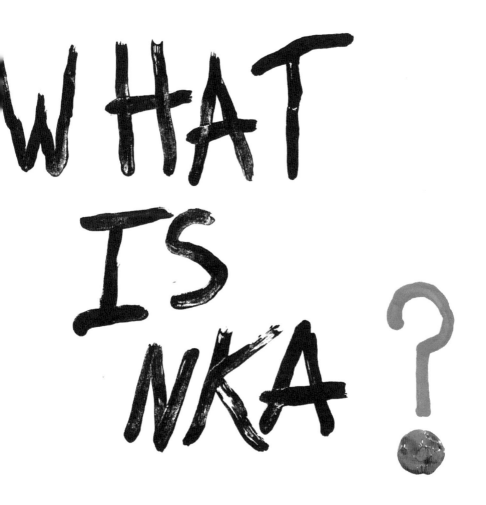

Written By:
Michael Uzoramaka Jonathan

Introduction

Life is very hard, especially for an African growing up in a foreign country. Sometimes you want to give it all up, but my faith in God kept me strong. I sit with you all today in front of my computer to write to you about my experience as an African growing up in Scotland. It was very difficult. But the Man Upstairs was very faithful. It will be a rollercoaster. I hope through it all you will be able to empathize and understand the struggles of immigration, disintegration and integration.

I do not write this to demean any culture or to make anyone look bad. I do this simply to tell the truth. As a great writer would say, 'Truth is originality'. The truth I speak of is not brutal, rude honesty, but the truth to find myself; to understand my name 'Nkà' and why God puts us through this journey we call 'life', however bittersweet it is.

Chapter 1

The Move From Africa

'Everybody has their own life to live'. This saying was the driving force behind many Africans who made their way to the West by any means necessary. For Nkà, a 30-year-old African man, it was no different. However, Nkà was an honest man and made his way to Scotland on an economy-class plane with his wife and two children.

He had spent his former life in Nigeria and grew up in a traditional Nigerian home. His father was a tough disciplinarian and his mother stayed at home to take care of the children. His father was rather cold and distant, but Nkà loved him because, as he would say, 'My father always provided food for us to eat'.

Being the middle child of the house isolated him and Nigerian culture made it more difficult for him to feel included. This was due to the culture taking its roots from tribalism, which made children workers for the house rather than people that should be loved.

This drove Nkà to leave home around the age of 16. He worked very hard to complete his education, walking to school with his talking shoes and shabby clothes covering his skinny frame. He graduated among the top of his class at university, married and had two children of his own. He slowly became a prominent man in the country, appearing on television, in newspapers and acquiring a large house in the bustling city of Lagos. The three-storey house had a coconut tree at the back, and a man guarded the tall gates and the three cars at the front of the house. However, this did not satisfy him. He wanted to make his mark in the West and the best way he could do so was to be granted admission to a university to complete his Ph.D. in Design and Technology.

At the turn of the century, he decided to make his way to Scotland on his own, but his wife did not want him to go without her and their two children. This led him to stay one more year until he had all the documents and registrations for his wife and kids. The laws in the UK stated that as long as he had a student visa he could stay in the country. However, his student visa had not arrived. Nkà then made another call to his university.

'Hi, could I speak to the head of the international student board at the university?' he asked.

After explaining his predicament, the university concluded that it was okay for Nkà to travel and stay as long as he had a visa and he was registered on their system.

That summer Nkà, his wife and children made the long trip to the United Kingdom. This was the first time he had travelled outside the country with his wife and kids, which made the whole experience exhilarating. He felt he was dipping his feet into the unknown. After several hours in the air, his son asked in a distressed voice, 'Are we there yet?'

The people on the plane burst into laughter as the child had said what was on everyone's mind. The phrase came from the movie with a similar name that Nkà's son had watched at the cinema before they boarded the plane. They finally landed at London Heathrow airport where the cool breeze was a surprise for his wife and kids. Of course, this wasn't his first time in the West, but Nkà couldn't help but feel that his life was finally going in the direction he had always envisioned. They got through the long walkway and gathered their luggage before being scanned to enter the main airport.

'Daddy, where are we going?' said Nkà's son, Malachi.

He was 5 years old, had a low fade cut, wore denim overalls with shiny black shoes and spoke with a Nigerian accent.

The Africans in Scotland called the tone Africans speak in a 'Freshy accent' – a reference to the common misconception that all Africans are 'fresh off the boat'.

'We are going to Joseph's house,' said Nkà.

'Who is that?' said Nkà's daughter, Sarah.

Sarah, aged 6, was slightly taller than Malachi. She wore beaded pigtails on her head, denim overalls and shiny black shoes. Her accent was no different from her brother's.

Nkà pulled out his Nokia 6236i, pressed a few buttons on his phone and brought the phone close to his ears.

Click.

'Hello, Joseph,' said Nkà as he began to laugh.

You were not Nigerian unless you laughed when calling a friend you had not seen in a while.

'How you, dey?' shouted Nkà. 'My wife dey here let me give you,' he said as he passed the phone to his wife, Ike.

'I'm going to go get a taxi,' said Nkà to his wife as he crossed the road leaving Ike with the two children.

His wife continued the conversation. She wore a long purple Nigerian dress and was slim in frame. Her skin was dark brown and she wore a gold wristwatch.

'Oya, let's go,' said Nkà as he walked towards his family.

Nkà carried his bags and some of the children's luggage.

'Okay we dey go catch taxi, see you later, bye ba-bye bye,' said Ike as she took the phone away from her ear and looked at the phone screen in front of her waiting for Joseph to cut it off.

She returned the phone to her husband and carried the rest of the luggage while leading Malachi and Sarah to the taxi.

They all got into the black cab, strapped on their seatbelts and made their way to Joseph's house where they would begin their journey: a journey with many lessons that would resonate with many around him; a journey that would lead to the meaning of his name.

Chapter 2

An Old Friend

In the taxi, there was silence as the children looked out the window and contemplated what they were seeing. The Nkà family were not poor in Nigeria, but it was clear that Lagos and Abuja could not compare to the beauty of London.

The taxi is very expensive, thought Nkà, looking worriedly at the meter.

He kept the concern to himself and looked forward to where he was going. As the taxi neared its destination, Nkà noticed a familiar African man with a woman and two children standing outside a middle-class home. The man was tall, stocky, wore a tan polo shirt with black outlines on the collar, black straight jeans and worn-out black leather slippers.

Nkà rolled down the window. 'Joseph!' he shouted.

Nkà and Joseph both broke into joyful laughter as the taxi slowly came to a stop.

'That will be £25,' said the taxi driver.

Ike and the two children get out of the car and were approached by Joseph and his wife Bunmi.

'Hi, baby girl,' said Bunmi as she waved and smiled at Sarah.

Sarah looked sheepishly at the ground and clung to her mother.

'Say good afternoon, Ma,' whispered Ike to her son Malachi.

Nkà reluctantly brought out money from his wallet and counted until he reaches the aforementioned price, then handed the money to the taxi driver.

Nkà turned to Joseph and they both give each other a strong handshake while smiling profusely.

'Good afternoon, Uncle,' said Joseph's two children.

'Good afternoon! Joseph, your children are all grown-up,' said Nkà

'Abi! How was the trip here?' asked Joseph.

'No be small ting. Taxi money dey high here,' said Nkà.

'Aa, it only be £10, how much dey charge?' Joseph said.

Twenty-five pounds,' Nkà told him.

Joseph widened his eyes in shock and shook his head. 'Dey cheat you oh.'

After Nkà and Joseph's short exchange they picked up the luggage and made their way into Joseph's home.

'Seyi, go and open the door,' said Joseph as he handed his son the house keys.

Seyi grabbed the keys and opened the door.

They walked through a well-maintained garden at the front and into the house, where they were immediately impressed by the neatness. Sarah and Malachi went into the living room and were taken aback by the large TV hanging on the wall, the rustic interior with the fireplace, and the clean, cerulean-blue fish tank at the side of the room, as well as the brown leather chairs. For them, it felt luxurious. No one was more impressed than Ike who gasped, awed at what she saw.

'The guest rooms are upstairs,' said Joseph.

Joseph took the family upstairs to their rooms. The guest rooms also had televisions, which was something the Nkà family didn't have in Nigeria. Even if they did have multiple televisions, they only worked with the luxury of continued electricity and sadly Nigeria wasn't too famous for its galvanism in that department. Almost every night the electricity around the street would cut out leading families to bring their generators out of storage. After a few strong pulls of the motor string, the electricity came on again. Unfortunately, there were times it didn't work and families had to light candles.

Nkà, Ike and their children had rooms opposite each other.

Joseph and Bunmi walked into the guest room

'We will be going out for dinner tonight. Make your-selves at home!' said Bunmi.

'Wonderful,' said Ike in a satisfied tone, which led them all to chuckle.

Joseph and Bunmi left the room and headed down the creaking stairs.

While unpacking in their room, Nkà broke the silence.

'You know the taxi dey cheat us,' said Joseph to Ike

'Ehenn?' said Ike.

Throughout the afternoon, the Nkà spend time unpacking and putting things in order for their outing later in the day. Joseph and Bunmi prepared to go out for dinner.

Malachi and Sarah got acquainted with Joseph's children. They were both the same age as Sarah.

'Do you like Bratz?' said Moyin.

'Want to see my toys?' said Seyi.

Safe to say, they quickly got along.

Chapter 3

A Better Life

Nkà was the first to get ready. He was a man who believed in looking his best but he was also an organized man, always a step ahead of everyone else. He headed down the creaking stairs while his wife began applying make-up to her face. He turned into the kitchen, which was rather small compared to Nkà's own in Nigeria. The kitchen was bright white and had smooth black tiles on the walls. The grey granite-looking dining table stood in the middle of the room and the end of the kitchen featured the stove and cabinets. The unkempt back garden was rather large and featured sculptures and landscaping that you would see in a park. Inside the kitchen was Joseph's wife who seemed to be finishing up her cooking. The aroma of ogbono soup filled the air. Moyin sat at the kitchen table eating an apple.

'Bunmi, where be Joseph?' said Nkà with a smile on his face.

Bunmi jumped and turned her head.

'I think he is outside right now getting the car ready.'

'I dey call you back,' said Joseph and put his Nokia 9500 in his back pocket.

'Bossman!' he said to Nkà.

Nkà and Joseph begin punching each other playfully. They hadn't seen each other for several years but had kept in touch by pager, phone, or email. They had been best friends throughout university and both had great dreams. After his marriage to Bunmi, Joseph had left Nigeria to work in London, leaving Nkà with his own wife and children.

'London be something else, Joseph,' said Nkà

'Na so. Naija economy be the problem. That's why many of us rather stay,' said Joseph.

Whenever Nigerians came together, they discussed Nigeria's damaged economy and corrupt politicians who stole from their own people. For many decades the economy had not improved. Nkà would always tell his children that, 'If Nigeria had better leaders, the country would be great. We have all the resources!'

Sometimes, they would blame the West for Africa's problems. A negative view of their country took precedence over the positive things and this encouraged many to leave their country to live a life that their own countries could not provide. If you weren't a doctor or engineer the possibilities of becoming successful or living a comfortable life without a job in politics was dim. This made the old adage of 'following your dreams' a point of ridicule.

Those who did stand out in the country and chased after their dreams were seen as outcasts. Nkà was different as he was one of the few to follow his dreams and succeed. Being a prominent businessman in Nigeria meant many people wanted a bit of his money. They felt they were entitled to his money. 'A black man's money is the community's money' was the mentality behind this thinking. If there was no easy money some contacted armed robbers.

One day Nkà's wife Ike had jumped in front of Nkà when one of these armed robbers pointed a gun at him when they made their way into Nkà's house. The constant barrage of people asking him for money and the huge responsibility of being a man in Nigeria discouraged him from staying within the country. That is when the opportunity of going to school in the United Kingdom had presented itself, and he'd quickly grabbed the opportunity.

The time to leave for dinner had come and all members of both families came outside of their house wearing their best clothing. Joseph owned a seven-seater so Malachi had to duck his head down the back car seat so the police wouldn't stop them.

The trip to the restaurant opened Nkà's family's eyes to more of London as they passed countless McDonald's and KFCs.

'Is there Mr Bigg's?' asked Sarah.

'No, there is no Mr Bigg's here,' chuckled Bunmi.

'Tantalizer?' shouted Malachi from the back of the seat.

'Your children like better food ooh,' said Joseph. Ike and Nkà laughed.

They finally arrived at the restaurant, which had a long line of mainly Africans standing outside, some in their traditional outfits. The restaurant sign had a distinctive black rooster. This image would edge within the memories of the Nkà's family.

Joseph looked for a place to park near the restaurant, then stayed to pay for parking while Ike led everyone else to the nearby restaurant. Not too much time passed before they were shown in by a slim African waitress, who wore a traditional patterned bandana, a black top, slim fit jeans and an apron with the company logo in the middle.

'Have you been here before?' asked the waitress as they took their seats.

'Yes, we have,' said Joseph.

'Great. Here's the menu,' she said and left the table to attend to other customers.

'What do you want?' Ike asked her children.

'Rice and chicken,' said Malachi.

Joseph ordered and paid for the meal, and the same waiter gave the children colouring books and crayons to occupy themselves.

'It's nice that they serve African food in this country,' said Ike.

'We always come here. Their food is very good,' said Bunmi.

The Angolan music mixed with African Highlife soothed the ears of everyone in the restaurant. It allowed those in the restaurant to feel like their country wasn't too far away and the non-Africans to feel connected to their roots. The decor had primary-coloured patterns that transfixed the eyes of young Malachi as he began to apply crayons to the pages of his colouring book, ignoring the original colour scheme of the design.

'The food will be here soon. I asked for extra corn for us,' said Joseph to Ike's delight.

Joseph took out his Nokia 9500 to show Nkà a business deal that immediately intrigued Nkà.

'Money no be small ting here,' said Nkà to Joseph.

Two waiters brought their food, balancing the plates on both arms. Joseph and Nkà begin clearing space for the incoming dishes.

The aroma of the chicken, flavoured chips, spicy sauce and corn swept blissfully through their noses. Malachi's stomach began to growl and his mouth began to water.

'Here's your pounded yam with egusi soup,' said the waiter as he placed a plate in front of Nkà.

'Enjoy!' said the waiters.

They began eating the wonderful food.

'Daddy, what's the name of this restaurant?' asked Sarah.

After chewing for a few seconds, Nkà answered: 'Ask your mum. You know I don't like talking when I'm eating.'

The food was quickly finished, although Ike didn't finish her food and asked for a takeaway bag to take the remaining food home.

They headed back in the car. Joseph puts on Smooth Radio urging everyone to relax. Malachi and Moyin fell asleep. Once again Nigerian politics was brought up in the car filling up the journey with great banter.

Once home Nkà and Joseph tucked their children into bed and got changed to head downstairs to watch the Nigerian football game on television.

'How does the cinema sound tomorrow?' asked Joseph.

The next day, they were back in Joseph's seven-seater, and went to church before going to the cinema on their final day with Joseph's family.

Chapter 4

Moving To Scotland

After spending time with Joseph's family, Nkà rented an apartment in North London. The house they stayed in was rather empty and there were no beds in the one-bedroom apartment. Nkà managed to buy a flatbed they could place on the floor for himself and his family to sleep on.

'I dey go to Glasgow to rent a place for all of us to stay,' he said.

'Okay, what about money for the children?' Ike asked.

Nkà took out a roll of cash from his wallet, counted it and gave a fair amount to Ike to last them the weekend.

That evening Nkà made his way to Scotland on a nine-hour bus journey carrying only a briefcase and some clothes. His children kept themselves occupied in London with the toys they'd received on their first day in the UK. Malachi walked around the area and saw two boys riding around on their bikes. The atmosphere and scenery were so different from Nigeria that Malachi thought he was in a whole different world.

At the end of the weekend, Nkà arrived to take his whole family with him to Victoria Coach Station.

'Mummy I'm hungry,' said Sarah as she tugged at her mother's dress.

Hours passed and the coach finally arrived. Many made their way into the bus and filled every seat. 'Our seats are at the back,' said Nkà.
The Nkà family made their way to the back of the bus and sat there. Ike took out her seasoned oven chicken from her bag and shared it with her children and Nkà. The smell wasn't too pleasurable for the other travellers.

The nine-hour journey to Glasgow excited Malachi greatly. He looked out of the windows with his eyes mercilessly glued to the window. His eyes flickered constantly like camera shutters as the landscape changed from mountain to forest. To watch the beautiful English landscape blend gently into the Scottish panorama was like watching the legendary Impressionist artists at work. The coach stopped multiple times and for the first time, Malachi and Sarah tried a McDonald's at the Manchester stop.

'What would you like?' said the disinterested McDonald's worker.
Ike diligently read the menu and tried to pronounce the food as well as she could, but to the dismay of the McDonald's staff, she just wasn't clear as Ike spoke in thick pidgin.
After nearly five minutes the worker finally understood what Ike was trying to order.

However, when the food arrived the waiter missed the medium fries and instead got two small fries. There wasn't much time to go to the counter again and try to change the order as the line was too long. She simply gave up and the children began to chow down on their fries. The interior of McDonald's fascinated the children: the colours, the colouring books, the sculpture of Ronald McDonald and the sweet aroma of processed food. Malachi greatly enjoyed his cheeseburger. It was like nothing he had ever tasted. However, he didn't like the pickles. Sarah especially loved her french fries; the salted oily fries were delicious.

It's like Mr Biggs, she thought.

Ike and Nkà had their own Big Macs. The taste of the food was beyond any fast-food restaurant in Nigeria.

The bus was about to leave, but Ike had disappeared. Nkà called on the phone. 'I dey buy sweet,' said Ike.

The driver turned on the bus's engine and lights but Ike still wasn't on the bus. A moment later, she walked out of the shopping mall. They were the second last people to get on the bus, before an elderly couple. One other traveller didn't make it back to the bus on time, but the driver had to move. Then they made their way out of Manchester and on to the motorway towards the Scottish Lowlands.

The sun gazed upon Alba for a few hours.

Alba is the Gaelic word for Scotland.

'We're nearly there,' said Nkà in a tired voice.

After a brutally but wonderful journey, the coach made its final stop at Glasgow Buchanan Street Station.

Everyone made their way down the coach and went to grab their luggage .

Nkà noticed that the children were very tired and weren't too keen on waiting too long. They rolled their bags to the nearest taxi rank to take them to their destination.

'We want to go to Glasgow University, please,' said Nkà as he shouted over the bustling noise of the bus station.

Like the first time they had taken a taxi in the West they crammed into the back of the small taxi.

The taxi driver began his meter but this time Nkà kept a close eye that he went the quickest way. The family was too tired to observe the Glasgow scenery, although the large Cineworld definitely caught the eyes of Sarah and Malachi. They reached Glasgow University, got out of the taxi, Nkà paid the correct money and the taxi left. The Nkà family had finally reached the home that they would live in for the rest of the year. They walked into the building, Nkà checked in and they walked into the lift, which took them to the eighth floor. What Nkà didn't tell his children was that they were living in student accommodation. The rooms only had one bed and a couch. The children slept on the couch while Nkà and his wife slept on the bed. The large windows looked over Glasgow and a sign peered at them saying 'Welcome to Scotland.'

Chapter 5

G-Town

After spending time with Joseph's family, Nkà rented an apartment in North London. The house they stayed in was rather empty and there were no beds in the one-bedroom apartment. Nkà managed to buy a flatbed they could place on the floor for himself and his family to sleep on.

'I dey go to Glasgow to rent a place for all of us to stay,' he said.

'Okay, what about money for the children?' Ike asked.

Nkà took out a roll of cash from his wallet, counted it and gave a fair amount to Ike to last them the weekend.

That evening Nkà made his way to Scotland on a nine-hour bus journey carrying only a briefcase and some clothes. His children kept themselves occupied in London with the toys they'd received on their first day in the UK. Malachi walked around the area and saw two boys riding around on their bikes. The atmosphere and scenery were so different from Nigeria that Malachi thought he was in a whole different world.

There was a lack of bedding so they had to use sofa beds for the children. The area was fairly nice with many squirrels and acorns. Both Malachi and Sarah picked up acorns and reenacted scenes from the cartoons they watched. It sometimes felt like a ghost town as hardly anything happened. Malachi remembered walking up long flights of stairs with his mum to buy food. Dinner was hardly a thing in Nigerian homes. They simply ate whenever they were hungry or when their mother had finished cooking, with the father taking the first helping. Their time in this flat didn't last too long and soon the family were moving again, this time to the West End of Glasgow. Their new apartment was a ninth-floor apartment with no lift. The rooms were very nice. As they lived on the top floor their rooms were refurbished attics with beautiful wooden ceilings, with Velux windows that bathed the room in natural light. The children were too young at the time to appreciate the rooms but looking back they had fond memories of the place. The kitchen, bathroom and living room were small compared to the bedrooms. Picking the children from school every weekday became difficult as both Nkà and Ike worked long hours, Nkà as a caretaker and Ike a cleaner and carer for an autistic child. Nkà enrolled the children in a school in the West End and they thoroughly enjoyed it, except the time Malachi was accidentally hit in the face by a bench. He wondered why many of the children were staring at him with a horrified expression.

Unbeknown to him his forehead was swollen. He was rushed to the school nurse's office and was given an ice pack. His body also itched when he sat beside the school heaters. Despite all this they enjoyed their time. After school, they were looked after by a blonde, flaky skinned white woman who smoked outside her apartment. She had two mixed-race daughters. Their father didn't seem be around. The lady took good care of Malachi and Sara and made their time adjusting to their new lifestyle easier It also helped that she lived close by and her daughters attended their school, the youngest in Primary 3 and the oldest in Primary 6. Malachi and Sarah were in Primary Months soon went by and a multitude of Christmas caro and advertisements began. Scottish winter had now set in White dust fell from the sky melting on the Nkà's family exotic faces. The children's eyes lit up in excitement.

'Snow!' shouted Malachi. The children stuck their tongues out to catch the snowflakes.

Living in Nigeria there was never snow due to the uninterrupted sun or refreshing rain. When their class-mates asked them about Nigeria's weather, Sarah and Malachi replied that, 'It snows mud' to the confusion of their classmates.

Their classmates wouldn't question them however a whenever an African spoke about their country's environ-ment, people tended to believe everything hook, line and sinker. In contrast, Glasgow was a very cold place and the Nkàs wore several coats to keep warm.

The children were always covered from top to bottom as Ike was afraid of them catching cold. During this time, she took her children on long walks through the Botanic Gardens and to the open markets known as 'Kashmirs', to buy the fresh vegetables sold by Asians and Africans.

It was Christmas morning and the children awoke to find presents under the tree. 'Aunty Stella gave you those,' said Ike as she pressed the buttons on her phone. Stella was the mother of the autistic child she looked after.

The only thing to excite them were packaged assorted puzzles. This trend continued for many years, as the children hardly got anything they wanted on Christmas Day because of the family's financial struggles, which led to the kids stealing things they couldn't have. Soon it was time to move once again. Nkà could not afford the rent and his time as a student was running out. He decided to move to Glasgow's southside. Within weeks, Nkà checked his children out of their school.

The up and down lifestyle of the family slowly affected the children's psyche but their young malleable brains tried to adjust to the circumstances.

The new two-bedroom, first-floor apartment they were now staying in was decorated in earthy tones and very modern. The kitchen and living room were open-plan. Malachi and Sarah stayed in one room that had sliding mirror-door wardrobes. Their parents had the second room closest to the front door.

The backyard was spacious and filled with cars belonging to the other tenants. The front of the apartment had a road that many cars, buses and cyclists passed along from morning to night.

For the first time the children got good cable TV. Malachi was enthralled by all the new animation he was watching on Jetix and Cartoon Network. The cartoons he watched would play an integral part in his life. At their new school , Sarah made many friends. The children walked to school every day as their mother watched from the window. The freedom encouraged their confidence and self-esteem. They came home and talked about how the school was right next to McDonald's and KFC.

In the same apartment complex were two African families that they became friends with. They would all go to KFC and the park with each other during the summer. KFC, with their seasoned breadcrumb chicken, was like a 5-star restaurant to the kids.

On Christmas Day, for the first time, Malachi and Sarah got the gifts that they wanted. Church members gave gifts to each other during the festive season. Malachi and Sarah's accents were still freshy but they quickly began to integrate into Scottish society. They also stopped stealing. Malachi adopted the saying: 'Stealing is telling yourself that you are poor'. Everything was going right: money wasn't an issue and the children even had a Nintendo DSI and were the first ones in their school to own such a console.

The Nkàs started to feel at home.

However, all that changed one morning when Ike was at home with the kids and Nkà was studying at his university library. A loud knock reverberated throughout the front door. Ike quickly stood up and slowly walked to the door. She peered through the spy hole. Her heart began to beat faster

Police? she thought

In a brave tone she asked, 'Who is it?'

'It's the Home Office. You are requested to open the door or we will have to enter forcefully,' said the Home Office worker.

Ike thought of the children and did not want any drama that could frighten them. She quickly removed the chain and unlocked the door.

As she opened it, she was able to clearly see the two Home Office workers: a short woman and a tall man dressed in police-like uniforms and black caps. They both had hardened looks on their faces. They made their way inside.

'Excuse me. I don't understand what is going on,' said Ike.

'According to our documents, you have over-stayed in the UK and will have to be sent home within days. Where are your passports?' said the man.

Fear immediately gripped Ike as she tried to compute everything that was going on.

'I yam sorry. Let me call my husband,' said Ike.

The woman walked into the living room to inspect the place for more people and was met with the cheerful and innocent faces of Malachi, Sarah and their African friend, Nica. Her face brightened and she began to speak with the children.

At the library Nkà got the call and immediately rushed home. Ike went into Nkà's luggage, as instructed by him, to look for their passports, as well as the university and travel information.

'We need to hold on to this for now,' said the Home Office man.

Nkà arrived home and tried to explain his predicament with the Home Office. However, it fell on deaf ears.

'The laws have changed recently. You can't stay here any longer,' they told him.

The Home Office left with their passports that day saying that they would be back in a week to begin the process of sending them all home.

Nkà prepared to leave the country for Italy as he had gained admission to a university there. Within days they began to pack. However, when Nkà went to the Home Office to collect their passports he was told, 'We don't have them.'

Nkà flew into a rage in the hope that it would lead the Home Office to send him back to Nigeria but it failed.

As he left the building, he heard a man tell him, 'Don't worry. It will all be fine.'

The man's words seemed to give him hope and as he looked back to get another look at him ... He vanished.

Nkà received his own passport but the Home Office couldn't find his wife's and children's. Out of desperation, Nkà prepared to leave Glasgow and go back to Nigeria himself but while waiting in line to take the bus to London he heard a quiet voice, 'Don't be selfish'

He turned around quickly. The voice was convincing enough for him to go home and be with his family.He decided to go to court and win his family's freedom back through the strength of the Lord. Going to court was a hard decision that would lead to a life that could only be explained as 'bittersweet'. His family would have to weather the continuous brutal storms of immigration.

Chapter 6

Bittersweet

The years went by and Nkà tried his hardest to shield his children from the consequences of his decision. He only spoke of immigration to his wife but the stress and pain was too much to bear. He had to quit his job as he could no longer work under the new law.

When he called the university, they also didn't know that the laws had changed and it was too late for them to do anything, so he had to drop out of university. To survive he received funding from his church. Soon enough the Nkà family had to move out of their apartment to another fifth-floor apartment in the far south of Glasgow. Nkà was ignorant of how rough and dangerous the new neighbourhood was. The constant arguments and trouble his family experienced would stay with them for many years. The family had moved around so much in so little time that Nkà felt like a pirate with a compass trying to reach all four corners of the city.

However, the freedom of a pirate had been taken away and now he was simply a criminal in the eyes of the law.

The children began to get used to seeing their parents argue and fight over money. The stress found its way to their children through objects like clothes hangers and fists.

'I'll blow your face!' shouted Nkà

A few months later, Ike's brother-in-law died. Her grief impacted the children as they saw their mother's distress and disbelief. Many family members died as the years went by, but without their passports they were unable to go home and attend the funerals. To take her mind off the pain, Ike engaged in self-destructive behaviour and indulged in snacks she stashed underneath her pillows and in her bags at night.

Ike took the children to various African parties to run away from her reality. She befriended many Africans who attended her church and would take her children with her to their houses. At one of these houses, Ike shared her distress with her closest friend Eve, who also had immigration issues. She had left Nigeria and moved to London first and then to Glasgow where rent was cheaper.

However, after divorcing her husband she was left alone to fend for herself and her 10-year-old daughter. She had lied to the immigration officers about being from Rwanda in order to not be sent back due to human rights laws, as Rwanda had recently endured a civil war.

She lived on the sixteenth floor of a white high-rise build-ing and moved multiple times because Glasgow was pull-ing down many high-rise buildings in the inner-city area.

Ike went to the east side of Glasgow to meet Eve and took Sarah and Malachi. They rode on the first bus for about an hour before getting off and walking through the dodgy neighbourhoods of Glasgow. She pressed the buzzer number 16 and was let in by Eve. They walked t the lift.

Two Glaswegian skinheads dressed in a reebok tracksuit with cigarettes firmly fitted between their index and middle fingers. One self-rolled blunt was also fitted between their ears. They walked out of the lifts. They growled at Ike and made their way outside the flat. Ike then entered the lift. Inside the lift was cramped and smelled of cigarettes from the passing residents. Some-times the lifts would jam and someone within the lifts would have to pull open the lift doors or wait for a me-chanic to come and save them. This immensely put off the option of taking a lift to anyone growing up in the inner-city areas of Glasgow. However, the higher the floor the less one had the option of walking up the stairs Sometimes, for fun one would take the lifts and another the stairs to see who was faster. A normal activity for those who were living below the working-class income. A the lift made its way up the G-force unnerved Malachi and Sarah as they felt their brain momentarily turn to mush. and went up to the sixteenth floor.

Ike knocks on Eve's front door.

There was no answer.

Suddenly, shouting and screaming developed on the other side of the door. Quick footsteps were heard .

Nica, Eve's daughter, opened the door with tears in her eyes.

'Good afternoon, Ma,' said Nica.

'Nica, how are you?' said Ike.

'Hi, Nica!' said Sarah and Malachi.

They both enjoyed going to Nica's house. She was a good friend and had different games consoles and games she would entertain herself with. Nica was also a very boisterous girl whose deeds would make her mother fly her into a rage.

Beating a child was a normal thing in an African household, an experience many first-generation children can attest to. The beating was often out of love and correction, but many times it was out of strained anger. Children walked to school with marks on their body but wouldn't say a word to the police out of fear. Some people said that this behaviour was fine as the Bible commanded them to, 'Spare the rod is to ruin the child', but they forgot that the Bible also mentioned that 'Fathers do not provoke your children to anger lest they become discouraged'. A child saying that they would call the police was a taboo and the child was often used as an example at African churches of what the 'Western children' were like.

It always begged the question of whether corporal punishment was effective.

Sarah and Malachi went into Nica's room, as Ike walked into the living room.

'Aaa, Ike! My sister, how you dey?' said Eve as she left the kitchen where she was cooking and walked into her small living room with a balcony at the left side of the room. The room looked like it was stuck in the 1980s: vintage chairs, carpets, a box TV and a fan on the ceiling.

'I dey fine,' said Ike.

'Make you sit down,' said Eve.

As Ike took a seat, Eve walks into the kitchen.

'Ike, coffee or tea?' asked Eve

'Tea. Three sugars. No milk please' requested Ike

Ike spent time watching television while Eve prepared tea within her small kitchen.

She brings the tea on top of a saucer to Ike. Eve pulls out a chair which was tucked underneath the glass dinner table that sat next to the outside kitchen wall. She crosses her legs and begins sipping her coffee. Ike sips her own tea and lets out a sigh. and Eve quickly noticed her nervous demeanour.

She has put on weight oh, thought Eve, as she observed her friend.

Some seconds passed and Eve decided to break the silence.

'How be your husband and the children?' asked Eve.

'The stress be too much,' said Ike.

Chapter 7

Immigration

Eve had been going through her immigration situation for seven years before she met Ike and so understood what she was experiencing. Many others had experienced immigration problems with the Home Office but what was most startling were the drastic actions many took out of fear and desperation. Eve told the story of a Ghanaian woman who she knew well, and who lived in an apartment similar to the high-rise Eve lived in. Every time she heard a knock on the door she hid in the bottom cupboards of her kitchen until the knocking stopped. On a grey-skyed Glasgow day her door was opened forcefully and out of desperation she leaped out of her fifth-floor kitchen window to the solid concrete. Her legs shattered and that led her to stay longer in the country.

Eve went on to tell the story of two couples who planned an argument when they had to sign at the Home Office.

'He's going to kill me!' shouted the woman.

The argument erupted to the point that the guards had to split them apart. The man was sent back to Africa whereas the woman stayed and claimed asylum so her children could eat. Without asylum an illegal immigrant was not taken care of. It wasn't long till the family was given their 'Leave to remain.'

Nkà began to see that families that split up were more likely to receive a leave to remain than those who did not, but he was determined to keep his family together despite temptations. He had once been offered the opportunity to marry a white woman at his work in order to receive his papers. This was a common practice and the woman who'd offered this to Nkà had done it for another African man in England. He was also advised to become an asylum seeker in order to receive money to feed his family, but he refused it all.

'Why should I become an asylum seeker when I came here legitimately?' Nkà asked his lawyer.

'Well, there's nothing else I can do,' said the lawyer.

The numerous trips to the Home Office to sign were exhausting. This was the procedure an illegal immigrant had to do by law, to inform the Home Office of their whereabouts in case they suddenly left without a trace.

It was a way to track each immigrant; as if they had become slaves in a foreign country. Nkà would hide his face so nobody would see them entering the building. African pride.

Many Africans he knew also attended the signing at the Home Office, but Nkà hid this side of his life out of embarrassment, even from his close family members. He did not want them to lose 'respect' for him.

Sarah and Malachi went after school several times a week and came home very late at night. They would wait at bus stops during the worst weather and were never given any transport funds. This continued until they went to university. Once they walked into the building they were stripped of their belongings. Bags and jewellery were first placed on trays before they walked through a metal detector. They also had to take off their belts and be scanned by the officer for any further materials that could harm others or themselves. They were then given a number and told to sit within a hospital-like waiting room before they were called by a Tannoy announcing their number. The waiting time could take hours, to Nkà's annoyance. The staff would sit opposite them with a Perspex frame shielding them. There would be a tray below to pass the number and immigration information they had or needed. After they had signed in, they were told when to visit again. Some of the staff who weren't too happy to see an immigrant would give the family extra days, whereas some of the nice ones would give them a week off.

One time a grumpy staff member gave the family a hard time making Nkà and Ike angry, to the point the young Sarah and Malachi cursed the man. To remedy the problem, during the Christmas period they gave the man a Christmas card. From that day forward the man did not bother the family anymore and was never seen again.

Malachi remembered visiting an African lawyer and experiencing vertigo as the reality of the whole immigration system dawned on him.

'I don't care if we get sent home!' he said apathetically.

It was enough for the boy to give up.

Many families were broken: children having to grow up without two parents; children growing up to be hooligans due to the lack of a father in the household – the silent desperation that would be masked with a fake smile was unceasing. The fathers of the household would develop hypertension and have to take medication to alleviate their stress, and mothers would develop diabetes and many health problems. This was the reality of moving to the land flowing with milk and honey. It almost represented the Exodus journey. What should have taken three days took forty years of suffering. However, Nkà had something that the Israelites also had – God's unrelenting mercy.

During this time, Nkà kept himself sane by fixing his mind on Jesus Christ. He left the church to a predominantly African church.

He built his relationship with God and made himself stronger through his words. While many families struggled he stood by Psalm 37:25 – 'I have been young, and now am old; yet have I not seen the righteous forsaken, nor his seed begging bread' – and Romans 8:28 – 'And we know all things work together for good to them that love God, to them who are called according to his purpose'.

Those two verses were his anchor and he vowed to never beg for money but work hard to provide for his family.

Chapter 8

Meaning Of Nka

What is Nkà? It was a question he was asked many times. Not having an English name invited so much intrigue about the meaning of 'Nkà'. He would answer plainly that it meant 'art' in Igbo, but that answer didn't seem to satisfy the questioner. It was as if they needed more. Nkà pondered this question himself in his bedroom at night just before he began praying.

'What is Nkà?'

Suddenly, a rush of ideas came to his mind and he grabbed his notepad and pen to jot them down – one was to find a job so he could feed his family. Nothing broke him more than not being able to provide for them and having to jump around questions such as why they couldn't go on holiday during the summer. An opportunity to work at a design firm came up. Fortunately, the design firm did not ask for his National Insurance number and were simply looking for skilled interns. Nkà immediately jumped at this opportunity and sent through his design portfolio. A week later he was given an interview.

He wore his blue tartan suit that he had bought in Nigeria and wore it for the interview. He kissed his wife and hugged his children goodbye. He made his way downstairs to take the bus to the city centre. The design firm was located in the West End of Glasgow. He got off the bus in the city centre and took the Bus 7 to near Kelvingrove Park. Knowing that the park was close to the museum, he decides to have a look at some of the art. He was nearly half an hour early so it was a good way to waste some time.

He walked into Kelvingrove and was immediately inspired by what he saw. The place was packed to the brim with people looking at art or simply sitting and chatting at their leisure. Nkà gazed at the artworks and walked into a small room that contained a painting that showed the narrative of 1 Samuel to 2 Chronicles, detailing the story of the kings of Israel. At the very end of the imagery, Jesus Christ was depicted as described by John the Beloved in Revelation 1:13, verse 16.

The vast intricacies of the painting captured Nkà's mind, soul and body. He walked closer to get a better view. The room he was in was bright red and the sun shining from the ceiling brightened the space and made the painting more prominent. Nkà was so enamoured with the painting that he did not notice that a woman was standing beside him, also looking at the painting in awe.

She broke the silence. 'Lovely, isn't it?' she said.

She wore a red tartan blazer with a matching skirt, high socks and smart shiny leather shoes. Under her blazer she wore a white jersey turtleneck. She was mixed-race and her hair had an exotic feature.

Nkà was taken aback by the lady's openness to talk to a stranger but relaxed and responded. 'Yes, yes, it is.'

'I come here all the time to see this painting. It's deeply profound,' said the lady, still facing the painting.

'I thought the same,' said Nkà. He took out his phone camera to take a photo of the painting.

The woman turned to her left to look at Nkà who had taken a picture of the painting. 'No flash photography,' she whispered.

Nkà looked at her in confusion as he changed his camera's settings to no flash. He couldn't understand why this complete stranger was talking to him.

'Are you an artist?' asked Nkà.

The lady giggled before answering the question

'No, I'm the director of Sunday design studios not too far away from here.'

Nkà immediately felt a small hint of excitement and nervousness travel throughout his body and stay in his gut.

Of all the people he could meet, he had met the lady who was supposed to be interviewing him today.

'I have an interview soon, so I'll leave you to it,' said the lady as she checked her watch.

She prepared to leave the room but stopped and turned back.

The strangeness of the encounter prompted her to ask for his name and to her surprise she realized that she had been interviewing him already.

The situation led them both to awkward laughter. 'What a coincidence!' she said.

It could only be God, thought Nkà as he smiled

'My name is Samantha. Nice to meet you, Nkà.' She walked over to him to shake his hand.

The interview at the design firm was scheduled in ten minutes and the encounter with Nkà made it impossible to make it back on time. Sabrina decided to conduct the interview in Starbucks, where they continued about how awkward it was to meet at a museum looking at the same biblical painting.

'I'm a Christian and this painting always gives me courage and stability,' said Samantha.

She sipped some of her coffee and continued. 'I always wondered what art was, but the answer appeared to me once I saw this painting.'

'I feel the same way,' said Nkà.

Nkà was surprised at the depth of the director and how similar they were in their world view. But in his mind, he couldn't shake the feeling that someone was behind all this. Not only had he not been asked for his work permit, but the director was also a Christian, who genuinely had a love for Christ. It was as if everything had happened for a reason.

However, now the questions turned to his design skills. The
director read through Nkà's portfolio and stumbled upon a
sentence written on the side of the page.

'What is Nkà?' she muttered.

Nkà's face dropped. I can't believe I jotted down that
question on the side of my portfolio! thought Nkà.

'Sorry, you can just ignore that. I don't know why I wrot
that there,' said Nkà awkwardly.

'Now I'm curious. What does your name mean? It
sounds West African,' Samantha said.

Now Nkà had to answer the question.

The question had been asked of him frequently and he
had only one answer – that it meant 'art' in Igbo – but this
time his answer on the question had changed. After lying on
his bed pondering his life up until that point, he had seen tha
there was something that God had planned for him. It was a
miracle that he and his family were still alive despite the year
of unemployment and hardship. Ideas flowed to him constantly and he took up his pen and notepad, and a poem had
come to him that he felt he had to express. He felt it was the
proper answer to his experience as an African in Scotland; a
good answer to the question.

Nkà let out a brief sigh of relief and smiled. 'If you flip to the
next page the answer is there,' he said.

The director smiled and out of curiosity flipped to the next
page. And as Nkà said, there was a poem.

She began to read.

What is Nkà?
To suffer is to love
To love is to let go
That we may reach
Satisfaction
Through Christ
Our Lord and Saviour

For God called us his Poiema
For to find Poiema
Is to find satisfaction
But at the garden He let go
He died for his satisfaction
His satisfaction he gave
Love
It starts and ends with us
The ones he loved
The ones he breathed his whole being into
The ones he suffered for
The only one
Nkà
His Church

The poem encapsulated an experience that only Nkà could understand. That weekend Nkà checked his emails and found that he had been given the job. He scheduled a family meeting and broke the news of the job making his wife and kids very happy. Although the family would spend another seven years without their passports they would always turn to God for solace.

In life we might experience many hardships, but always remember that to balance the bitter with the sweet opens us up to see what is sandwiched in the middle – Jesus Christ's love.

The AfroScot Experience

Written By:
Michael Uzoramaka Jonathan

Introduction

'Why's everyone smoking?' said Uzor, in awe of the smoky water vapour emitting from the mouths of the many Scottish people surrounding them as they disembarked from the plane. It was still summer, but the Scottish heat did not rival the peppery African sun. Many foreigners emigrated from their struggling countries for a better life. However, over time, many could not shake the bittersweet feeling of doing so ... The struggle continued in their new home; an imagined land flowing with milk and honey.

If you don't understand the past, you will never anticipate the future.

Chapter 1

Childhood

Uzor's journey through adolescence and integration into Scottish culture had begun. The bright-red sun scorched Uzor's proud Nigerian skin as he got out of the van and looked up to see the new apartment that his family had moved into. First Uzor scoped the area. It was fairly clean. A strange, elderly, short-statured woman sat in front of her porch. She wore muted clothing and was smoking a cigarette. She noticed Uzor, looked at him with a friendly grin and continued smoking. The lady occupied the ground floor of the building.

The van men started taking items upstairs led by Uzor's father . Uzor, still looking around curiously, noticed that the apartment complex all looked the same. It was a four-storey complex that continued to the end of the street. A large woman in a flowing dress, with embroidered, black rose-petal designs on top, approached Uzor.

She asked him to carry two nylon bags holding a few items upstairs. Uzor looked up, startled to see the black twists in her hair.

'Mum, I thought you had a different hairstyle before we got on the van,' he said.

'It's a wig!' said Uzor's mother aggressively. Uzor quickly saw her reaction as a sign he should hurry upstairs.

'Chibuzor, house key!' said Uzor's father as he walked down the stairs, which were each large enough for two feet.

On either side of the stairs metal railings coated in maroon paint curved several feet away from his father who was at the centre of the stairs. Uzor could tell they had been painted many years before from how chipped and rusty they were. His mother rummaged through her handbag pulling out chocolate bars, tea bags and pads before locating the house keys.

'How could I forget the key? I'm sure they're waiting upstairs. I'll go up,' said Uzor's mother. His father manned the van while Uzor and his mother walked up the stairs towards the entrance. A slipper edged the door to keep it from closing. Before they walked into the building, Uzor looked at the elderly lady near her porch. She looked back at him with sceptical eyes. Uzor then looked up to see the apartment number.

'226,' he muttered to himself. He would never forget that number.

They walked up the stairs which were located on the left side of the apartment. The apartments were strange as there were no doors located on the first floor. They could only be accessed from the outside. A door was located on the right-hand side of the first floor and would take a couple of seconds to get to the door which provided access to the backyard. The dim first floor smelled like an unfinished construction site. Dust moved into different spaces on the unkempt stairs, where spiders reigned supreme. Uzor noticed the chipped and neglected red blocks of paint smeared on the walls. At the top of the stairs a bright blinding light came from the window and highlighted a beautiful flowerpot on the window sill, clearly placed there by residents. The window framed a beautiful view of Glasgow City Centre. Even though they were several miles away from the city centre the grand exterior of the Armadillo, one of Glasgow's natural treasure, stood out. The higher they went, the more the cleanliness of the stairs began to fluctuate. The second floor was neat, whereas the third floor was dirty. They finally reached the fifth floor where their flat was situated. The top of the building was the most unkempt. Uzor snapped back into reality.

'Sorry for the wait! Here are the keys,' said Uzor's mother to the van men.

She opened the door to reveal a house with no carpets. It was all hardwood punctuated with plenty of nails.

The walls needed a fresh coat of paint and the place was generally empty. A strong smell of dampness reached Uzor's nose. It was very different from the student housing he had stayed in before his family finally got this place.

Uzor left the shopping bags at the entrance and made his way around the house checking the individual rooms. The room on the right-hand side of the entrance was the largest, while the room across from it was the smallest. That would be his room. He made his way along a tiny corridor, towards the tiny bathroom to his left, which was extremely small for a family. However, Uzor was still excited and expressed his joy about the move. He left the bathroom and headed towards the living room. The kitchen was on the left-hand side of the living room and too small for a dinner table but for Uzor it was like he had just walked into a McDonald's.

Suddenly, the sun came out from behind a cloud. Uzor looked behind him to the living-room window. But he was too small to look through it, so he lifted himself onto the window sill.

'Wow!' he said as his eyes gazed at mature, green trees and spotted various birds that soared in the sky. In the distance wind turbines seemed close as their blades spun slowly like a jazz tune. He marvelled at the view.

The honey-like sun warmed Uzor's eyes and face as it began its evening descent, smearing the sky with iridescent colour, as if nature had its own palette knife.

Uzor's attention was drawn to various high school-aged boys dressed in tracksuits, with rough hair, driving down the road on illegal dirt bikes.

Cool! I want to try that! he thought.

'Uzor!' shouted his mother

'Yes, Mummy!' Uzor responded.

'Stop misbehaving, Jor, and go downstairs to help your daddy!'

Uzor took heed and rushed downstairs, with a faint smile on his face, excited about the adventures ahead.

Chapter 2

Primary School

Primary school had started and Uzor's parents had enrolled him in a school situated behind the apartment block. Uzor was excited to be going to school as he knew this was a chance to make new friends. At first his mother walked Uzor to school but soon he walked himself as his parents were occupied with renovating the flat. On walking into his classroom Uzor noticed a young boy with bright platinum hair, who smiled at him. Uzor took his seat and shortly his teacher introduced him to the rest of the class. Playtime came and Uzor hung around by himself. The playground comprised a wide concrete field and the only places for entertainment were the shed, the front entrance area and the football pitch, which was the main playground for the primary school kids. Uzor appeared lost until he was approached by the platinum-haired boy. He looked at Uzor with a friendly smile and held out his hand to shake. Uzor returned the gesture

'Ma name is Junior. We saw ye by yerself... Ye can hang aroond wey us, if ye want,' the boy said in a strong Glaswegian accent, common to those who lived in impoverished housing schemes.

Uzor couldn't say no to the request, as deep inside, this is what he was looking for. He was naturally a quiet and shy boy, who liked to keep to himself, but he desperately wanted some friends.

'Yeah, I'll hang around with you. Thanks!' he said.

Junior's face lit up. He walked across the playground towards a group of boys. Uzor followed. Junior began introducing Uzor to his crew of friends. Jake was a short-statured boy whose smile contained yellow teeth that contrasted with his pale white skin. Then there was Scott, a taller boy, the spitting image of Billy Ray Cyrus with his long mullet. They both introduced themselves to Uzor.

'Here, do ye play fitbaw, Uzor?' said Scott.

'Obviously he plays fitbaw. He looks lit Pele,' said Jake.

Jake's words sent all three of them into laughter except Uzor who didn't understand the comparison. Junior decided to invite Uzor to football after school at the pitch at 5 p.m. so they could get home for dinner at 7 p.m. Uzor swiftly accepted the invitation, excited to have a new set of friends he could play football with. No child should spend his days alone.

Several days had passed and Uzor, growing ever restless and filled with youthful energy, decided to embark on his awaited adventure. His mother, knowing how much of a handful her son could be, allowed Uzor to leave the flat as long as he came home on time. Uzor went out carrying his old and ripped football which needed pumping up. He wore a simple t-shirt and a pair of shorts and had decided to keep his hair uncombed, curly and puffy. He went out and saw the elderly lady once again, this time wearing a black rain jacket and carrying a newspaper, as she opened her garden gate. She smiled at Uzor and he smiled back, ran downstairs, and began kicking the football along the street. As he did so, he noticed various Scottish kids his age looking at him strangely, as if he was an alien. Uzor ignored them and kept kicking the ball till he got to the end of the street. He turned left and walked up the hill towards the school football pitch. The streets were fairly quiet, but seemed to hold an air of danger, like a Neo Rauch painting. As he reached the football pitch, he saw Junior and his friends playing a game of football. Uzor wanted to join in, but saw no way to enter the school grounds. How did they get in? Uzor wondered. He shouted to his friends to get their attention.

'Awright Uzor!' said Junior

'Awright! How did yous get in?' Uzor asked.

Junior pointed towards the gate and encouraged Uzor to climb up it in order to enter the playground.

Uzor wasn't an experienced climber but was anxious to give it a try. In order to give Uzor some confidence, Junior climbed over the gate effortlessly onto Uzor's side.

'See, it isnae scary,' said Junior

After seeing Junior's demonstration, Uzor climbed the gate surprisingly well, which gave him Uzor the confidence to climb over the next gate to reach the football pitch. They were playing penalties with Jake kicking the ball into the net and Scott as a goalkeeper. They were talking aggressively about a recent Old Firm game. Uzor had no idea what they were talking about but constantly heard

'Celtic' being talked about in the best light.

'Wan touch,' said Jake and passed the ball to Uzor

Uzor, completely dumbfounded by what 'wan touch' meant, decided to take a shot into the football net. It wasn't a bad goal. Jake was perplexed at Uzor's antics but shook it off.

He's new, he thought.

Junior decided to get a new conversation going, while practising his skills.

'Which team do ye support?' he asked, his eyes staring straight at Uzor.

'Celtic or Rangers?' added Jake

Uzor was completely confused about who these teams were and quickly remembered the Old Firm conversation he'd overheard, with Celtic being talked about in a good light.

With lightning speed, he responded, 'Cel ... Celtic?'

All three of them look at each other for a few seconds before running up to Uzor, and raising him on their shoulders and rubbing the top of his head with their fist.

'Yassss!' shouted all three of them

'He's a Tim!' screamed Junior

His hair feels like a carpet, thought Scott

Uzor didn't know what was going on, completely oblivious to the age-old Glaswegian football tradition. Growing up in Glasgow meant many things, but first and foremost, you had to pick a team. You were either a Celtic fan or a Rangers fan and it was mostly the dream of the young to become football players and play for their respective teams. The ones who would become players for Celtic or Rangers were deemed legends.

To Uzor, football was just a hobby, a way to make friends and play rough as a boy, but to Junior and many other boys in Glasgow, becoming a footballer was 'Their dream,' as Junior said with a sparkle in his eyes.

Growing up in the area where Uzor lived, if you were not a Celtic fan you were doomed. Uzor got hold of the ball and started kicking it around the field, prompting the boys to join in. They decided to play penalties and thenplay against each other. Uzor was having the time of his life, working up a sweat and sliding around the field as he saw on TV. It began to rain and the street lights turned on signalling that it was time to head home for dinner.

The boys grabbed their football and climbed over both gates.

'You're sound, Uzor. Shud come oot mere,' said Junior as they parted ways.

Uzor began going out more with Junior, Jake and Scott to play football. They began teaching Uzor different tricks, which he learned with fervent determination. However, his zeal could not hide the fact that he wasn't talented or skilled at the game.

'Stop skinning yerself,' said Jake, making fun of Uzor's odd move of passing the ball through his own legs so he could turn round and get away from a player who was trying to get the ball from him. However, Uzor continued to play, showing he wasn't too bad of a defender as long as he could stick his legs out and take the ball from an opposing player. After intense hours of playing, Junior stopped the game for a break. They had brought snacks with them and drank Lucozade. Uzor had only brought a bottle of water filled with granulated sugar. Suddenly, their attention was directed towards the other end of the pitch. Uzor watched in amazement as players from the upper primary years appeared, and proceeded to play football effortlessly.

'They're in the school team,' said Scott.

Joining the school team was the most prestigious position you could have at primary school, and an automatic path to popularity. All the girls wanted to be with you and all the boys wanted to be you.

It was also a way to get the teachers to like you. However, fo
Junior, it was more than that. It was a way for him to become
what he wanted to be: a professional football player. Watchi
the boys play reminded Uzor of the football games he had
watched with his father, who was a huge Chelsea fan. Being a
Chelsea fan usually meant you supported Rangers in Glasgo
but Uzor routinely argued that he was a Celtic fan to stop the
barrage of insults from his fellow classmates.

'There are tryouts for the football team this week!' said
Scott excitedly.

Hearing those words from Scott moved Uzor to action.
As a young boy who'd always felt he had to prove himself in
some way or the other, the football team tryouts were the
perfect opportunity for him. Although he knew he wasn't the
best player in the school, he decided to have a go. Further
encouragement from his parents bolstered him even more.

The next day Uzor and his father decided to go to the
pitch and practise football. At a young age his father had bee
very good at football and had even played for his local footb:
team in Nigeria – a team called 'Rangers', which was an inter
esting coincidence.

His dad showed Uzor a spinning kick that sent the ball
spinning to the corner of the net. The trick was to hit the side
of the ball with the underside of the foot. Uzor tried but he
just couldn't get it right. A bunch of boys slightly older than
him walked onto the pitch.

The weather was slightly cold as autumn was approaching. As the boys watched him play they taunted him every time he missed his shots. Uzor and his father ignored the taunts. Suddenly, two boys from his primary school arrived. Uzor knew the boys. One of them was wearing a Barcelona football strip, and they challenged Uzor and his father to a game of football. Uzor felt nervous, but the presence of his father gave him confidence. They agreed to play.

'First wan tae five goals wins,' said the boys.

The boys who had taunted Uzor earlier, sat near the goalpost and watched.

The game kicked off and Uzor's father got off to a good start and scored two goals. However, when Uzor got the ball, he failed to shoot the ball into the net, completely missing the target every time, even though there was no goalkeeper. Eventually, one of the boys passed Uzor to score their fifth goal. In their excitement they begin teasing Uzor for missing his shots despite no goalkeeper being present. It didn't help the fact that it was an eleven-a-side goal post.

As Uzor left the pitch in embarrassment he looked to his left to see the other boys look at him with a devilish grin as they taunted him, particularly a blonde-haired boy with a mullet. However, in his eyes Uzor thought he could read the faint sign of compassion. Maybe the boy was just jealous of his relationship with his father or it was something else.

Uzor's father began scolding him for missing the shots, but Uzor didn't take this to heart knowing that his father also wanted to win. The rain beat down on Uzor's face as he spent more time inspecting the ground than what was in front of him.

Once at home, Uzor took to drawing to take his mind off the loss. He saw drawing as something he could never lose at. And it was when drawing that Uzor decided to use the football team tryouts as a way to prove himself to everyone that he could win at football.

The next day at school Uzor practised his football at playtime. As he walked to the bottom of the school football pitch two girls, one of them named Sarah, tried to catch his attention. As soon as Uzor looked at them, they began demonstrating Soulja Boys' 'Crank That' dance. The demonstration was comical, making Uzor laugh.

That was weird, he thought .

The school bell soon rang and Uzor was in class when he started to get glancing looks from Sarah. She was in the same year as him, but he had not really noticed her before. She had bright ginger hair, which flowed in an impressive mane down her back. Her face was covered in freckles and she had bright blue eyes. His friend Jake leaned into him as they sat at their tables.

'Here, I think Sarah fancies you,' he said Jake.

Uzor's body temperature rose. However, with his chocolate-brown skin his bashfulness could hardly be noticed.

Sarah, her friend Lucy, Junior and Scott sat at the same table to the right of Uzor. Both their backs were glazed with the sun penetrating through the school's windows. Thoughts of Sarah ran through his mind all through class time and he began drawing Sarah's face in his English jotter. The teacher left for a few minutes, giving Jake the opportunity to ask Uzor for help with a question. He was suddenly surprised to see that Uzor had been drawing someone that looked faintly like Sarah.

'Uffftt!' Jake shouted. Everybody's attention turned towards Uzor's table as they tried to understand what all the commotion was. Scott got up from his table and looked at Uzor's jotter. At first, he squinted, but suddenly the image became clearer.

'Sarah, he drew you!' Scott bellowed. Uzor was mortified as Scott lifted up his jotter and showed her the drawing. Suddenly a loud 'Aww' burst through the room and Sarah's freckled face immediately grew warm. It was not too long after that, that they started dating.

Soon enough Uzor was the talk of his primary school year. Sarah's mother worked at the school and always smiled at Uzor, sometimes encouraging the talk of 'marriage' from his fellow classmates. Everyone seemed happy about it – Everybody but Junior.

For some reason, since Sarah and Uzor had begun dating, Junior had started treating Uzor like an outsider, avoiding Uzor and calling him names in class.

At football he would encourage insults about Uzor skills and made fun of Uzor's lack of sports gear. Uzor's family wasn't financially stable and his parents were more focused on getting food on the table than buying Uzor sports gear. But if you weren't wearing Nike or Adidas, you weren't considered cool. You were considered a 'jake' or a 'scag'. However, Uzor still decided to attend the tryouts for the football team. All the kids had fancy football gear except Uzor, who wore a simple t-shirt and cheap jogging trousers that stopped just below his ankles. In Glasgow they called the style 'budgeed'; was a derogatory term for those who wore poorly fitted trousers with hems that stopped at the shins.

The PE teacher led the tryouts. He was a tall lanky man with dyed short black hair. He always wore a blue button-up shirt and black trousers with smart shoes. It was quite cold outside so he had a large puffer jacket on with a fur trim around the hood. He watched each player intently but ignored Uzor as he lacked the natural talent that the rest of the boys had. Junior was obviously a genius. However, despite his own poor performance, Uzor noticed he had improved since the last time and was still hopeful that he could enter the school team. A week later the results came in and Uzor ran towards the A4 sheet of paper stuck on the walls of the PE corridor showing who was in the school football team.

He read to the end of the paper but didn't see his name so he scanned it again. thinking he had misread it. but to no avail: his name could not be found. Every one of his friends got in but he did not. This loss would haunt Uzor for the rest of his life. His one chance and he'd blown it.

From that day on, Junior's insults and coldness increased. Uzor slowly started to avoid playing football, opting to stay indoors and hang out with Sarah, but that also didn't last. Uzor began to play games with Sarah, avoiding being upfront with his feelings for the girl and insulting her. He would decide to break up with her for fun and then immediately say he was joking. One day at the end of the school day Uzor decided to break up with her again, but this time Sarah had had enough and for the first time, Uzor experienced a broken heart as Sarah slowly drifted away from him and started to spend more time with Junior, who said to him, 'I don't even know what she saw in you. You're ugly.'

Those words damaged Uzor's self-esteem even more. In his mind his life was crumbling.
On his way home from picking up butter at the nearby convenience store, he decided to have a chat with an elderly neighbour; a large man with a balding head that revealed age spots, and thin-framed glasses. He had taken a liking to Uzor as he reminded him of his late son who had been trampled to death in a Celtic game stampede.

He always recounted how he hated God as God had taken away his son. Uzor's parents were devout Christians and attended various church services several times a week. Uzor didn't quite understand what Christianity was all about at his young age.

The old man decided to buy Uzor the most recent Celtic football strip along with brand-new boots in his size. Uzor was oblivious to how rare and expensive the boots were as they had only come out. This was the first time Uzor had had such trendy clothing. He thanked the man and began wearing the strip and boots to play football. He naively thought this would gain the favour of his fellow classmate, but Uzor wasn't aware of the spirit of envy in the area where he lived. He decided to go to play football at his school. Two boys began talking to him and decided to play football with him. Uzor decided to play without his boots because they were very tight and it would take him time to break them in. As soon as Uzor turned his back and walked to the other side of the pitch to get his ball, the two boys ran away with Uzor's football boots. In a panic, Uzor ran around the area looking for them, but the boots were long gone. Strangely, he never saw the boys who'd stolen his boots ever again. Uzor continued wearing his old footwear and avoiding the old man for fear of him asking about the football boots. From then on, Uzor became a target for bullies at his school who saw his skinny and shy demeanour as a weakness.

Primary 6 boys chased Uzor as soon as school finished and waited for Uzor to get close to them so they could catch him and beat him up. This led Uzor to walk the long way home. He avoided telling his parents what was happening. This continued for several months until the bullies got tired. In the meantime, Uzor stayed at home, only leaving for school and for church with his parents.

Sunday came and the family got dressed. Church was a huge thing for Africans. They would dress to the nines in suits and dresses. Elsewhere this was called 'Sunday best', but for us it was just to celebrate Jesus Christ's love for us. Dressing badly was an insult to the Church and to ourselves. Uzor was always dressed by his mother, who used her eye for tailoring to execute the boy's dapper outfits, by mixing the right garment with the correct colours. At church, Uzor spent his time walking around marvelling at the interior of the building. He sometimes ran out the back where there was an open field for picnics. The car park was a couple of feet away from the field, separated only by a black metal fence fixed in ancient bricks. Church to Uzor was an adventure. On the opposite side of the church was a bowling green that always seemed to be empty on Sundays, and behind the church rose a massive warehouse.

It was soon time for the main service and Uzor went into the church to sit next to his parents. The main service hall was dark with only the altar lit up.

It had a classic gothic appearance and was plastered with modern decorations. The musicians on the altar picked up their guitars, drum sticks and microphones.

Uzor watched with interest. The church Uzor was filled mainly with white Scottish people and the noise in the room increased as more members of the church arrived to take their seats. Uzor took his seat as the service commenced. The boy next to him was engrossed in a game of Pokémon dungeons on his Nintendo. Uzor had never played the Nintendo and his father couldn't afford one, so seeing a boy around his age freely playing during the service intrigued him. The only console Uzor had played was a GameCube, which at the time was considered 'ancient'. He began to take peeks at the game and soon enough began asking questions. Brian decided to give Uzor a shot and soon a friendship began to bubble.

Every time Uzor came to church he looked for Brian to continue their discussion of video games and their exploration of the church. Brian was Scottish and had short ginger hair – a 'short back and sides' was a popular hairstyle for kids their age. He had a stocky build and wore a tanned t-shirt with tracksuit bottoms, and a pair of Heelys, on which Brian would demonstrate his skills in the church toilets and on the ramps for the wheelchair users.

One day at the end of the church service Brian invited Uzor to his home.

Uzor was at first hesitant to accept the invitation as he remembered how it had gone with Junior, but he quickly shook off the thought, seeing this as a way to go on another adventure and explore new things – a normal thought for a child in primary school. Everyone was thirsty for adventure in their own way. Uzor asked his parents if he could go to Brian's house. Luckily for Uzor, Brian's mother and Uzor's mother talked regularly at church and after having a chat with his Brian's father, they allowed him to go to Brian's house. Uzor's excitement rose as he rushed to tell Brian the news!

Chapter 3

Brian's House

The next Sunday, after the church service was over, Uzor prepared himself to go to Brian's house. He searched around for Brian but couldn't find him, until he decided to go outside to the front of the church. A church member opened the front entrance with a warm smile. There was something about Christians that always stood out to Uzor and that was their genuine joy that illuminated every-thing. Church was a safe haven for him. On the left side of the building was a long path that led to the back of the church and the car park. Brian and another boy seemed to be in deep conversation with each other. The boy had taken his t-shirt off to reveal a crimson sunburn mark on his back.

'I got this while on holiday in Spain,' said the boy.

Brian looked in amazement. Uzor decides to interrupt. It was one of the rare times he had seen a sunburn mark. As an African, seeing a mark like that was an extremely unusual event.

The melanin in his skin protected him from the sun and the only evidence that the sun had somehow affected him was the further darkening of his skin. In general, an African with dark skin would rarely have sunburn. Uzor impulsively pressed his finger unto the mark. He just couldn't help himself. The boy winced in pain, but tried not to say anything and stay calm. He left them and entered the church leaving Brian and Uzor together.

'That was my cousin! It's not good to slap sunburn. They're sore,' said Brian.

'Oh,' Uzor said apologetically

Brian father came out of the church and looked at the two boys. 'Are we heading home now?' said Brian.

Brian father nodded. He was a tall Dutch looking man and wore a long brown coat over a blue shirt, slim khaki trousers and simple brown office shoes. Large round-framed glasses sat across his face. His father walked towards the small car park. Brian and Uzor followed and crossed the road looking both ways for oncoming vehicles. His car was a polished, black Land Rover. Brian sat in the front with his father and Uzor sat in the back settling on the left side of the car. Brian looked around.

'Where's–?' said Brian,

'Your sister and mother are at home,' said his father.

Brian's curiosity was quenched. His father started the car, and turned on the radio. Uzor tried to relax. Brian passed Uzor a stress ball that his father always kept at the side of his car.

While Brian pressed on talking about the stress ball, Uzor couldn't help but notice the view of Glasgow outside the car. Glasgow had many unbalanced roads, potholes and buildings for rent or for sale. There was a Blockbuster Video shop that was closing down. He remembers a conversation he'd overhear where his parents had talked about how quickly the world was changing. Of course, at his young age he did not quite understand what that meant. The world felt the same. Uzor began to notice the traffic lights and examined how they worked. It seemed like the traffic lights were working against them as the car constantly came to a halt every time they came near a crossing. It wasn't too long until they were driving towards the motorway, which was a strange sensation for Uzor to drive on, because it felt like a moving picture. The other cars thundered around the ground like a silent earthquake, with Uzor safe inside the car.

They entered a tunnel with orange lights that shone brightly, and seemed as if they were travelling through the inside of an orange. The lights pulled Uzor in, mesmerizing him; a euphoria that lasted a moment and then quickly vanished as they merged from the tunnel. The Kings of Leon's song, 'Sex is on Fire' roared through the car speakers. Listening to it felt taboo, but Uzor couldn't resist, and he moved his ear closer to the speaker in the car door, taken by the music and the atmosphere. They soon left the motorway and a sign caught Uzor's eye: Clydebank.

They were soon surrounded by lakes and trees, as if they were in the countryside, but what really caught Uzor sight was the massive emerald-green mountain that stood proudly in the foreground, as well as the fields, hills and lochs. This was all a dream to him. Were they still in Glasgow or somewhere else? He didn't want to ask the question or know the answer. Instead he enjoyed the view.

Finally, Brian father took one last turn and stopped in front of a house. The music stopped immediately and Brian's father got out of the car, followed by Brian. This signalled to Uzor that it was also time for him to leave the car. The first thing Uzor noticed about Brian house was that it was very posh, compared to his own. Flowers and trees seemed to delight in the air and the soft wind caressed his face gently, as if he was on a beach. Brian's house had a garage and another car parked outside. Both sides of the house were enclosed by a green hedge. There was no apparent front garden, just well decorated con-crete. Brian's father delved deep into his pockets for the keys and opened the front door. As soon as the door opened, the first thing Uzor noticed was what a mess it was: coins, socks, clothes, and everyday items were all over the floor, doors and shelves. The house was split into two parts. There were stairs on the right side of the ground floor that led up to three rooms, behind a white railing. The second part of the house was downstairs on the left side of the ground floor and featured two rooms on the right and a bathroom on the left.

Brian's father made his way downstairs. Brian had a huge smile on his face, clearly excited to be with his friend Uzor. They went into one of the rooms on the right closest to the stairs, which appeared to be Brian's room. Brian guided Uzor to a white desktop computer in the middle of the room, typed in 'Club Penguin' and showed Uzor all the different tricks and mechanics of the game. He then led Uzor to a massive sofa riddled with what seemed to be dirty washing. Brian turned on the PlayStation and began to play Guitar Hero. Uzor found it hard to play as the tunes he had to sync with were too fast for him. However, he still enjoyed it.

Quickly growing bored of the PlayStation, Brian turned on his Xbox 360. With so many consoles and games at his disposal, Brian could afford many options – a luxury for someone like Uzor. He found it difficult to get a handle on the controls because he had never owned an Xbox, because his family couldn't afford one. Uzor quickly remembered when he'd been was in Curry's a few years earlier and he'd wanted his father to buy the latest console – the PlayStation 3. After looking at the price, his father had called one of the sales staff, who for the first time made Uzor's family financial position clear to Uzor, when they said, 'It's £299, not £2.99.'

As a result, Uzor often lied to his classmates about owning several gaming consoles, only getting caught when his poor playing skills were exposed.

Brian decided to play Sonic and then Super Mario Galaxy. Uzor focused deeply on the games but didn't have the same natural aptitude as Brian. As time went on Brian grew bored, as is normal with kids their age, and headed downstairs to the kitchen. The kitchen was well lit with natural light coming from a large window that overlooked the unkempt back garden. It featured various toys, footballs, water guns, all hidden among the tall grass, and a wet trampoline. Uzor and Brian took their seats in the middle of the room at a white marble dining table. Brian's mother, a short ginger-haired woman sporting a Chanel-type suit, served them French toast. She was an extremely reserved woman and hardly spoke, but when she did it was with a quiet aggression that could rival Uzor's mother. It was the first time Uzor had eaten French toast, surprised by the odd mixture of egg and bread. Brian mother placed two Mr Men and Little Miss books by Uzor. He flicked through them, fascinated by the pops of colours and odd shapes that the characters sported, which reminded him of cartoons he watched. The simplicity of the artwork intrigued him.

Feeling ever restless, Brian decided to go into the garden for a shot on the trampoline with Uzor. The unkempt, forest-like backyard made Uzor uncomfortable because many bugs roamed the grass. Nevertheless, Brian's easygoing presence took his mind off the issue. Brian showed Uzor various somersaults and backflips that Uzor was too afraid to try, fearing he would break his neck.

'Let's go on bikes,' he said.

They went out the front to take a shot on Brian's bicycles, but Uzor had no idea how to ride one. It also did not help that the bikes had no hand brakes and could only be stopped with your feet. Brian decided to teach Uzor how to ride a bike. They walked out to the front of the house and decided to practise going down steep pavements. Uzor looked around and was taken aback by the beautiful homes in the neighbourhood, a far cry from the apartment housing Uzor was used to. The empty roads and pavements gave Brian the space to teach him and for Uzor to feel comfortable. After falling off a few times, Uzor finally got a hang of the bike, so Brian decided to push it even further, taking him on a trip around the area, introducing Uzor to his friends. One of the boys Brian knew had a rough look to him and had overly broad shoulders. He looked like one of the boys he knew back home. Another one of Brian's friends was a Scottish boy around their age, who had a mischievous, anxious look to him. They stopped at a nearby park and played on the swings before getting on their bikes again. Brian and Uzor continued their ride around the area and passed many houses, unafraid of anyone or anything. As Brian rode in front of him, Uzor began to see Brian as an older brother. His natural leadership and social skills were leagues above Uzor's and he admired him for that.

Sensing that it was time to head home, Brian cycled faster. Uzor followed and observed several things.

They arrived back at Brian's house and his mother and older sister came out of the house on their way back to church for the evening service. Brian's sister was incredibly beautiful. She had brown hair and blue eyes, was already at high school, and carried herself with an air of sophistication. Uzor had never seen a girl as beautiful as her. He did not mention his attraction to Brian 's sister to anyone.

Oblivious to Uzor's wandering thoughts, Brian headed upstairs to his bedroom and started to show Uzor his collection of toys that were in a box at the bottom of his bunk bed. Uzor was astonished by it. Brian had several toys that Uzor had always wanted, particularly a deck of Pokémon cards, but Uzor's parents couldn't afford to buy him Pokémon cards. Uzor often cried, and had brooding mood swings whenever he was denied the cards, which led to his mother buying a pack of cards unwillingly. However, the pack only had three cards in it – poles apart from a full deck. Uzor still treasured his cards.

Brian was reluctant to give Uzor any of his toys as he was very possessive of his things, but sensing Uzor's admiration of his cards, he generously gave Uzor a couple of them, which instantly made Uzor's day. Brian got changed for evening service and made his way to the front door where his dad was waiting. The day with Brian had allowed Uzor to taste a different life he had never experienced before.

With one last look at the scattered interior of Brian's home, he made his way to the Land Rover.

On the motorway, Uzor once again gazed at the bright neon lights on distant buildings. To him the darkness of the night made the faraway landscapes resemble millions of rainbow dots, all working in unison to illuminate the city. In Uzor's opinion, Glasgow could rival New York at night. They arrived at church and both boys made their way from the reception to the café, to buy gummy snakes and spend the rest of their time inside the church's gym where they practised roller skating, until Uzor fell and landed on his right hand, pushing his elbow joint further up his arm and locking it in place.

Chapter 4

Uzor's House

For a couple weeks Uzor had to wear an orthopaedic cast as advised by one of his mother's friends who was a nurse. Uzor, now confined to his house, spent most of his time watching cartoons when suddenly a thought came to him: Why don't I ask Brian to come to my house?

Several weeks had passed and Uzor attended church, where he saw Brian.

'Why don't you come to mine?' said Uzor excitedly

Brian's parents struggled to agree as Brian was wearing a Rangers strip.

'I've coached many boys and when a Celtic fan sees a Rangers strip it all goes wrong!' said Brian's father.

Luckily, Brian's mother had packed some spare clothing for her son and eventually agreed to the invitation. Both boys were ecstatic and spent their time adventuring around the church and playing video games.

Uzor's mother would take them home but, in the meantime, she had choir practice.

Uzor's mother had finished practising, but always took an extra hour to leave church. She was notorious for her long conversations with members of the church. Eventually, she called Uzor and Brian, and they walked to the nearby bus stop five minutes from the church, passing a Blockbuster on the way. Several minutes had passed and no bus was in sight, so the bored boys start to recite the song

'Oigy oigy oigy ... in a trolley.'

Uzor's mother caught on to the meaning of the song

'Stop singing that!' she said aggressively. Silence filled the air before their bus arrived. Children were free on the bus and the boys ran to the back where they began making funny noises excited about the adventure that awaited them at Uzor's house. The spontaneity of child-hood blinded Uzor to what the next few hours with his friend would bring, completely changing the course of the young boy's life.

They got off at the nearest bus stop across from their house. Uzor's mother immediately got into an argument with the bus driver. This was a normal thing with Glasgow buses: bus drivers were known for their impatience and rudeness. Uzor's mother tried to contain her anger as she led the way to the apartment. Once home, they entered Uzor's room and Brian was surprised at how small it was. He looked around expecting a Xbox or PlayStation, but was soon disappointed when Uzor brought out his Game-Cube.

Brian accepted the situation, and they began playing various street football games, NBA Street Vol. 2 and Shrek SuperSlam; games that kept them both occupied. Brian focused on the game ignoring the mouldy walls near Uzor's bed. Boredom soon filled the air and the boys made their way to Uzor's backyard – a small concrete-filled space with various neighbours' many cigarette butts. On either side were bins: one for recycled goods and the other for general waste. There were also wired clothing lines held up by maroon, rusted metal poles. In front was a gate that led to a large rusty fence that separated Uzor's primary school from his house.

It was not too long until Brian started to feel restless. Out of desperation, Uzor offered to take Brian around the area and took his ripped and flat football along with him, heading to his school's football pitch. Brian struggled to climb the gate as he was slightly bigger than other boys his age. However, after a few more tries he finally climbed over and beamed at his success.

Sensing Brian's irritation, Uzor quickly started a game of football, but before they could properly get into the game, boys from the area interrupted it and began harassing them. One of them even provoked Brian into a fight. Brian didn't want to look weak, especially in an unfamiliar area, so he began to talk back to the boys, which only increased the tension.

'Let's play a game of guppies,' said Uzor.

The boys looked at each other and laughed.

'It's called cuppies, ya fanny,' one of them said.

Uzor knew that saying anything in return would only exacerbate the situation. The boys decided to play along with Uzor. However, the decision did not work out in Uzor's favour because the boys began to cheat, grabbing onto Brian's top and dragging Brian down whenever he got the ball. The blatant bullying got too much, and Brian decided to leave the pitch. Uzor ran after him, forgetting his ball on the pitch. They make their way back to Uzor's house where they were treated with oven chicken made by Uzor's mother. They ate on the floor in Uzor's living room, as most Africans do not have dining tables in their houses.

When they got their food, they ate wherever it was free for them to sit, which was the living room. Brian was not used to this type of food and ate it reluctantly, deciding to leave the chicken, which was still covered with small bits of poultry. As an African, witnessing Brian not devouring the pieces of chicken was highly disturbing. Uzor continued eating his chicken, chomping on the bones when he could. At this point, Brian was fed up and ready to go home. He looked at the house clock counting every tick and tock. A loud buzz suddenly went off in the apartment. Brian, hoping it was his father, was delighted to hear that it was. He quickly grabbed his stuff and said goodbye to Uzor with no smile or joy on his face.

Chapter 5

Inclinations

Uzor went back to his room and remembered that he'd left his football at his school pitch. He ran out of the apartment, down the street, made a sharp left turn towards the pitch and found it empty.

Where's the ball? he wondered.

Uzor searched frantically for the football while he had flashbacks of his stolen football boots. Unsuccessful, and with his head staring at the ground, he made the difficult decision to head home. As he reached his street his spirits lifted as he noticed Mark, an older boy from his primary school, with his ball. He was dribbling it towards him with a friend beside him whose height made it clear that he was in high school.

'That's my ball,' said Uzor, determined to get the ball and not prepared to leave without it. Mark held the ball tighter.

'Naw, it's ma baw. Ah hud it aw day,' said the older boy.

Uzor and Mark's friend knew he was lying. Suddenly, Mark's friend rolled his eyes

'Gee um it,' he said.

Mark started to argue with his friend, but his friend repeated,

'Gee um it.'

With pressure from his friend, Mark handed over Uzor's ball.

The scene and the righteousness of Mark's friend struck a chord within Uzor. He would never forget it. At home, Uzor went straight to his room and thought about what had taken place.

Sunday was a complete mess, he thought. He knew his only friend, Brian, was never coming back; his primary school life was a shambles; and he did not seem to fit into anywhere. When he did fit in, he was soon shunned. Uzor did not say anything to his parents, but kept everything to himself. Slowly, Uzor recovered and his childlike optimism came to the forefront. He knew he just had to find something he could dedicate himself to, but he just didn't know what.

Chapter 6

Finding Purpose

Summer was approaching. Uzor's parents decided to change church, opting to attend an African church situated in the West End of Glasgow. A child's imagination can take them away from the unpleasant reality of life, into the world they most love and connect with, alongside the characters in their cartoons. Uzor began spending more time alone watching cartoons and playing with his stuffed toys, stretching his imagination as far as the universe. He was fascinated by the drawings of the characters and he would find a sheet of paper from his father's shelves and draw the characters. Knowing his parents' financial situation forced him to start drawing his own Pokémon cards using his coloured pencils for the Pokémon, normal pencil for the card information and scissors to cut out the rectangular shape of the cards. This soon consumed his time during the summer. It was not long until Uzor was filling bags with his drawings.

He had been fascinated with drawing from a young age. His uncle was an incredible draftsman and after he came back from work, he would urge him to draw Spiderman. Uzor loved Spiderman and watched the movies with Toby McGuire with religious zeal, and even cosplayed. He swung on ceiling lights, breaking his nose in the process when he slammed into walls unable to stop the momentum. A few minutes later his uncle would have a sublime drawing of Spiderman using red and dark blue biro. Uzor would become extremely excited and immediately ask him to draw another one. Just the very act of creating something out of nothing fascinated him. It was as if, in that moment, his uncle was creating something out of nothing. Maybe this view of art tied in with Uzor's religious background as God was said to have created the earth out of nothing within six days. To Uzor, God was the original artist.

Uzor continued to draw throughout the summer and his parents encouraged their son's efforts after watching him spend countless hours with his pencil in his hand and paper in front of him. His parents watched him moaning about the poor finish of his drawing. 'I can't get it right,' he cried.

This was the beginning of his perfectionist approach to art. His parents began buying cheap art supplies and sketchbooks for their son to practise. When they could not provide any more for Uzor, his father would instead lend an ear to Uzor's wild ideas.

This slowly built up Uzor's self-esteem. Soon enough, his whole school class caught wind of Uzor's talent as his artistic skills outshone everyone in the class. One student was even noted asking Uzor, 'How did you do that?'

When he drew several characters from the cartoon, Ben 10, no one could rival his skill. It was not long till everyone wanted Uzor in their team when it came to art. Despite this, Uzor still felt dejected. At his African church, he felt he had to conform in some way. Art was not something that was highly acclaimed in the African community. It was seen as frivolous and any mention of such a thing was quickly shut down. Uzor soon started saying he wanted to be a software engineer to avoid seeming strange. However, his parents' encouragement spurred him on and he continued to draw.

Chapter 7

African Childhood Friend

A new African boy joined Uzor's primary school. He was a year older than Uzor and was called Fela. His family had just moved into the area. Fela sported a large afro and his face always had an anxious look. He was taller than Uzor and wore shoes that were far from trendy. Fela and Uzor soon became acquaintances, walking home together and discussing the latest cartoon or anime they had watched, as they were both voracious readers of Manga. It wasn't long till they started visiting each other's homes. Their families seemed to be in the same financial position as their homes were nearly identical. The only difference was that Fela's room was a complete mess and seemed to get worse every time Uzor entered it. Fela had a big interest in music. He could play the bass guitar and often participated in his church's band, where his father was the pastor.

Fela and Uzor's parents had similar faith and beliefs. The only difference was that Uzor's parents encouraged his talents whereas Fela's did not.

This led Fela to lead a double life whereby he appeared hip and cool around Uzor but passive and timid around his parents, as if he had entered a cage and his parents had the key. Fela's parents wanted him to become a doctor but deep down he wanted to be a musician. The mere thought of spending his whole life as a doctor distressed him. It just did not fit his personality. Uzor was not aware of Fela's passion for music until they visited a guitar shop in the city centre. Downstairs was full of bass guitars. Fela played a tune on one of the guitars and astonished Uzor with his ability. 'You're really good,' he told Fela.

Their friendship was tested one Friday at Golden Time, which was an afternoon to play and have fun. They were playing with Beyblades, a spinning toy that was taking kids in the United Kingdom by storm. Uzor and Fela were the first ones to catch wind of the trend. The other kids had laughed at them calling them childish, even though they were all still in primary school, but they weren't put off. Their intense passion for the spinning toys rubbed off their classmates, encouraging them to join in eventually. Every Golden Time was now an event and several boys would line up for the Beyblade tournament set up by Uzor.

To Fela, Uzor was a breath of fresh air, someone he could relate to. It was the same for Uzor, and their friendship strengthened. Fela soon left for secondary school leaving Uzor to begin his final year of primary school.

It was at this point that the internet became a regular conversation point at school. Many of the boys began to talk about pornography and sex. Puberty was also regularly talked about and it became a trend to make fun of boys who hadn't grown any hair 'down there'. Uzor tried to avoid the conversation, but he soon shared in the chat. During sex-education classes many of the boys, still immature, would joke about in class and make wild, outlandish jokes. One of the boys asked, 'Is the white stuff in pee, sperm?'

Time flew by and it soon reached the end of Primary 7, when the school arranged for their class to go to the cinema to watch Spirited Away. Serendipitously, Uzor already knew about the movie, but the experience of watching it with all his classmates left a lasting mark on him. The loud vibrant colours, cinematography and art direction stood out even more and he immediately began taking mental pictures of each scene. The film embodied art showcased in a way that he had never seen before and an animation quality far ahead of all the cartoons he immersed himself in. It was as if something deep bubbled inside him. He didn't understand what it was, but the only way he could articulate what he was feeling was by drawing.

Although everyone else in his class complained about how odd the movie was, Uzor loved every moment of it.

'That was very strange,' said his class teacher.

Uzor kept his thoughts to himself, only telling Fela about them.

He decided to attend the school's Burns' Night Supper, eating haggis and listening to his classmates' temporary choir.

Uzor was nervous but excited about leaving primary school. A trip to M&D's theme park took place in June. M&D's was small but seemed big to a primary school kid. It was a refreshing time away from school. The best rides were at the far end of the park while the children's rides were at the sides. Secretly everyone wanted to go on kiddies rides but backed out owing to the fear of being ridiculed. However, Uzor didn't care and headed straight for the spinning teacups. As the sun started to fall on a windy June evening, it was apparent that an era was soon coming to an end. M&D's was a proper send-off.

A chapter closed for Uzor and a new one opened, in which Uzor would have to understand himself even better in the ruthless world of secondary school.

Chapter 8

Summer

During the summer, Uzor spent the majority of his time with his uncle, Segun, who was a bachelor. He lived beside the Clyde River in the city centre. Segun wasn't his real uncle but a member of the African church Uzor's parents were now attending. Segun served in the children's department of the church. Uzor's parents were fond of Segun, which led to Uzor staying at his house for a few weeks in the summer. Uzor loved the place. Segun had all the latest gadgets, three rooms, two of which were empty, and a flat-screen television attached to the wall of his bathroom above the bathtub. The bathroom remote allowed you to also connect to the television in the living room. As you can imagine, this was quite exciting for Uzor.

From the living room, the view of the River Clyde and the cascading waves of water that slid off the sides of the passing boats inspired and calmed him.

At the time, Facebook was becoming popular and Uzor spent the majority of his time on Segun's laptop, chatting with his classmates. He talked to them about what they were doing over the summer and their feelings regarding the first year of secondary school. Most of them replied nonchalantly.

Uzor was generally lazy and he grumbled about cleaning, calling it 'torture'. To combat this, and apply discipline to Uzor's regiment, Segun forced Uzor to practise maths, wash the dishes and clean the rooms in return for them going out in the evening to the Quay. Despite this, Uzor and Segun got along. He was a role model and like a second father figure for Uzor. Segun always wore shorts, a Ralph Lauren top, his hair in dreadlocks and a perpetual smile on his face pronounced by his glistening white teeth. Uzor remembered the games he played with his uncle vividly. They would compete to see who would get downstairs the fastest: his uncle would go down the stairs whereas Uzor would take the lift. Mysteriously, Segun would always win despite taking his time. They were only three floors up, but this always surprised Uzor.

How does he always win? he wondered.

The smell of the apartment corridors was a strong reminder of the student housing, where his family had lived before his parents' big move. Summer was ending and Uzor had to head home. However, he wanted to do one last thing: his uncle was going to take Uzor to JD Sports to buy new trainers.

This would be the first time Uzor would experience having his desired pair of trainers bought for him. He did not want them because he genuinely loved the trainers but because he knew they would ease the pain of going to school and being bullied as nobody would, at least, slag off his shoes. After receiving the trainers, Uzor returned to Segun's house every summer, and got a new pair of trainers every time. Segun's house was his retreat.

Chapter 9

Secondary School

It was the first day of secondary school. Uzor had to attend a class, but was 15 minutes late due to him thinking the class started later. On arrival, he was greeted with unfriendly looks, as he was the only one to walk into the class late that day. After the first period, the students had to go downstairs to have their pictures taken for their brand-new Young Scot Card. Uzor sat nervously and got his picture taken.

Secondary school was totally different for Uzor. First, he cut his hair off, leaving him with a 'baldy', which was ridiculed by the classmates who had joined him from his primary school. Uzor was embarrassed and tried to ignore the taunts, secretly wishing for his hair to grow back instantly. Second, was the size of his secondary school, which was spacious even though it held less than 400 people – small size compared to a larger secondary school in Glasgow called Holyrood which held around 2,000 students.

The corridors were wide with a strong stench of drying wall paint and sanded wood, with the latter most pronounced in the woodwork department. Uzor almost felt at one with nature. For many, the canteen was the best part of the secondary. They had signs for burgers, pizzas and drinks – a sight unseen at primary school, which gave secondary school food a false sense of grandiosity.

Another thing that was instantly be recognizable was the bold behaviour of the students. Third-year students were infamous for their antics, always clashing with teachers and senior years. Fifth- and sixth-year students were notorious for their ill nature. A couple of weeks into first year Uzor got into an altercation with a group of fifth-year students during lunchtime in the canteen lines. Uzor was in front of them but the fifth-year student decided to queue-jump. Annoyed, Uzor decided to barge in front of them. This angered the students, leading to them shout and vocalise their disdain for Uzor's actions.

'First years,' said one of the dinner ladies in a patronizing tone, with a sly grin across her face.

Uzor was extremely sensitive and these actions hurt his feelings. He left the line to cry in his hiding space under the school's stairs. After 10 minutes, he wiped his tears and went back to the now empty line. Unbeknownst to Uzor, an African fifth-year girl had been watching the drama earlier on. She was in the line next to Uzor. She turned to him, and looked at him with nurturing eyes. Her name was Eniola.

'Are you okay?' Eniola asked. She was a tall, slim, Nigerian queen.

Uzor simply nodded.

Racism at the school was rampant. You could count the number of Africans at the school on one hand, which made each African at the school an easy target.

Uzor soon got into various fights and petty spats due to ignorant racist comments – 'Chocolate Spread', 'Nigga', 'Black Bastard' – and students singing lyrics with racist words were everyday occurrences. Uzor was skinny and slightly timid, which made him even more of a target. His lack of athleticism led many of the boys to berate him. Fortunately, he was allowed into the school football team, but only played one game and was never picked again. It was as if he had been picked out of pity.

Soon enough, Uzor was getting into countless arguments with the teachers and having a generally bad time at school. His grades fell dramatically, and his parents were too occupied with their finances and putting food on the table to pay attention to their son's failure to make friends and his poor academic performance. That soon changed when his English teacher began reading sections of a book that had so many racist, derogatory statements and phrases that it led other students in the class to snigger and chuckle. Exhausted and embarrassed, Uzor told his parents, who immediately called the school and set up a meeting with the head of Uzor's year.

The book was then cancelled from the school's reading list. It was a victory for Uzor, but his English teacher never forgave Uzor and spent the remainder of his time in her class breaking him down. Not feeling liked by other boys and his teachers, Uzor tried to find happiness by befriending the girls. But his personal hygiene and clothes were so poor that the girls avoided him. He used the same school bag and shoes over and over again to the point his feet outgrew them and began to squeeze under the tension. His bag became the topic of discussion at the canteen tables. If you did not wear Nike, Adidas or a designer brand you were considered a 'jake'. Uzor could only remember receiving puzzles for Christmas from his mother's friends, but nothing from his parents.

Uzor did as much as he could to not get bullied, but the fact was, he was African and did not come from a well-to-do family, which made him hard to ignore. Considering the area was rough, Uzor just could not understand why they valued expensive things so much. Most of them could not really afford what they had. If it was not obvious already, Uzor wasn't popular in secondary school where looking good and popular was everything. So, being associated with Uzor was not great.

Uzor decided to start hanging around with Junior, his first friend at primary school. Junior's attitude towards Uzor had changed and they quickly became friends again. Junior had slimmed down a great deal over the years but still retained a certain amount of baby fat.

Junior's cousin, Louis, had moved to France, but then returned and joined their secondary school. He was feared and respected in the neighbourhood after doin' two notorious delinquents. One of them brandished a knife but Louis still stretched both of his arms to the side.

'Mon then', said Louis, showing his lack of fear.

This courageous or stupid act gained him respect. He had grown up in the area and naturally knew everybody. He could fight well and was extremely confident. He always had the latest clothes and gadgets and the girls liked him. He took a liking to Uzor ,but always made sure to let him know who was boss through his offhand racist comments. The comments were not hard-hitting but slowly dug into Uzor self-esteem.

However, Louis still treated Uzor like a friend, stuck up for him at times and made sure they got lunch together. He liked Uzor's calm demeanour, quite different from the majority of boys in the area. This started to irritate Ciaran, Louis's friend, who despised Uzor. Looking to dominate, he began insulting him, leading to Uzor joking about Ciaran's mother. This angered Ciaran and he used that as a crutch to justify his hatred towards Uzor. Uzor could not understand why Ciaran hated him. Mum jokes were repeated all the time between classmates and Ciaran usually laughed it off, but towards Uzor it was different. The truth was that Ciaran was very insecure and hated feeling inferior, especially to someone like Uzor who he called a 'worst cunt' – an unpopular boy or girl.

One day, Ciaran and Uzor were out together but Uzor had to ask his parents if he could stay out longer. When at the front door of Uzor's apartment, Uzor's father was the one to open the door and gave Uzor permission to continue staying outside. While this was a simple moment, it exacerbated Ciaran's hatred and jealousy of Uzor because he did not have a loving father or a loving home. Louis and Junior left for a school trip, leaving Uzor vulnerable. An argument between Uzor and Ciaran kicked off. Uzor tried to avoid a fight but many of the boys at the school provoked the situation, adding more fuel to the fire. Classes were boring and a fight was what many of the boys looked forward to everyday. Fighting at the school got so bad that the head teacher had to have a full meeting with all the boys in his year. Uzor knew that a fight was what Ciaran wanted, as Ciaran always had it in for him and would wait in the toilets or boys in Uzor's class would approach him.

'He's waiting in the toilet,' said one of his classmates.

Uzor ignored the taunt and stayed in the canteen to eat his regular roll and sausage. Ciaran became restless and left the toilets. He sat at the same table as Uzor, provoking him repeatedly and looking at him with murderous eyes.

'You're a bitch, ya ugly bastard', said Ciaran.

Uzor ignored the insult once again. The boys around them began shouting, 'Oooooh'.

'Calm down, boys,' said the canteen wardens.

The canteen wardens were not astute enough to pick up on the rising tension between the boys. A fight was brewing and its momentum was not decreasing. The ringing of the school bell and moving of the various students gestated the dilemma. It was the third period and everyone was heading to the English department. Ciaran decided to take the same route as Uzor. He walked in front of Uzor as they reached the final flight of stairs before English. Brimming with anger he turned back towards Uzor and began his onslaught of insults. Uzor calmed himself down but the pressure from his classmates' laughing and shouting really stirred the pot.

'Square go,' said Ciaran with a serious tone.

This time he could not be ignored.

Uzor felt his body temperature rise and he became numb. He felt that his hands were now tied. He couldn't run away from a 'square go' as doing so would make him a constant victim. As a male running away meant you were a 'shitebag'. Uzor's adrenaline skyrocketed. He felt it first in his ears as they grew incredibly warm, piping hot. Everyone immediately cleared the space

'You're a bitch!' sniggered Ciaran.

'I don't like when people call me that,' replied Uzor.

Uzor and Ciaran squared up to each other and started throwing punches at each other. Uzor wasn't an experienced fighter but he knew how to throw fast jabs, which prevented Ciaran from weaving and throwing accurate punches.

He was under pressure to perform. Uzor continued punching, losing himself in the moment. Everything was going too fast. The noises around Uzor disappeared as his adrenaline peaked to a level he had never felt before. His heart raced faster and he continued throwing his punches, feeling them dig into Ciaran's skin. Suddenly, Uzor felt his nose become extremely warm.

Schoolteachers ran out of their classes and broke up the fight. Uzor was held back by one of his taller classmates, James, who he knew from primary school. He looked at Uzor with a concerned face and put his arms on either side of Uzor, planting his palms on a nearby wall, to block him. Uzor had his back against the wall. He looked down and started to see drops of blood on the ground. He moved his hand in front of his face to check his nose, wondering why James was looking at him that way. His nose was pouring blood. He was exhausted and on an emotional high. He did not know how to react.

'Uzor!' said his drama teacher, surprised to see Uzor, a quiet boy, in a fight.

Everyone slowly dispersed and Uzor was taken to to the English staffroom by his English teacher who gave Uzor a tissue.

'It's okay. Things like this happen' said his English teacher.

Her posh English accent destroyed any semblance of empathy.

Uzor rubbed the tissue along his nose, wiping up the blood. He was then taken to see the head of his school year and was suspended. On his way home he met his parents taking groceries upstairs. His father looked at him in confusion.

'Aaa, why are you home early?' he asked.

'I got into a fight.'

'When are you going to learn?' said his father as he shook his head.

Chapter 10

Drugs And Alcohol

Third year started and the drugs and alcohol began to spread.

'I am never going to take drugs or alcohol,' was a sentence many children said, but by secondary school those views quickly changed, as a result of wanting to conform and peer pressure. And so, many teenagers began experimenting with drugs, sex and alcohol. At first it started off as a 'one sip' or 'one draw', but as the stresses of puberty kicked in, they became dependent on such substances. Some tragically succumbed to the pressures and took 'bad yin', leading to their early deaths. A year didn't go by without news of someone dying in the neighbourhood through illegal substance abuse. Uzor could not get his head around why. His parents never smoked or drank and he never wanted to.

At the right side of the school there was a forest section where the students would 'sook' buckets. Buckets were a cheap way to inhale marijuana.

They would cut a plastic bottle in half, pour some water into it, place marijuana into a screw and heat up the water with a lighter. The vapour would be 'sooked' – or inhaled – leading to a temporary high. It was an easy way to take drugs and it was mostly associated with 'Neds' – hooligans or louts – as the boys who took drugs were considered wayward. However, that view soon changed when Junior and Louis looked around for Ciaran. They asked around and got news that Ciaran was hanging around the bushes near the school. They make their way to the bushes, with Uzor in attendance

'Wit you dain, Ciaran? I'll tell your ma,' said Louis angrily.

'Then you're a grass,' said Ciaran.

Being called a grass was the worst thing to be called in Glasgow. It implied that you were not to be trusted and was also a very uncool thing. Grassing to an authority figure was the same as conversing with the police. The 'grass' card was used to keep people in line, stopping anyone from doing anything. The only ones who wore the 'grass' card proudly were the 'worst cunts'.

'I'm no a grass,' said Louis.

Seeing that Ciaran was fully aware of what he was doing and not wanting to look like losers, Junior and Louis left the bushes.

That day deeply affected Uzor. The drug mania was infectious, and it was not long before Junior and Louis began participating.

They were difficult to avoid. There was not much to do after school. Football became repetitive and most boys by this time had given up their dreams of becoming professional football players, owing to a lack of opportunity and positive role models. Crime began to rise in the area: there were break-ins, drug dealing and stabbings. Many youth workers gave presentations at the school, teaching kids about the importance of street smarts.

'Make sure you don't put all your belongings in one pocket, in case of future muggings!'

Despite all the craziness around him, Uzor stayed sober, being one of only a few who stuck to their childhood views.

This led Uzor to remember Fela.

Chapter 11

First High School Party

Fela was still at secondary school, but as he was a year older this discouraged communication between Uzor and himself. Fela also had his own group of friends. At the whole-school assembly, in the canteen, Uzor spotted Fela. He now had cornrow braids, was very tall, but still had an anxious facial expression. He walked around in his school blazer and sat at his friends' table. Uzor from afar knew, from Fela's uncomfortable demeanour, that he was also just trying to fit in.

The last school bell rang and Uzor separated from Junior and Louis. They both headed down the street while Uzor waited for Fela outside the school gates, looking forward to their reunion as he felt they had plenty to talk about. The group of boys Fela was hanging around with walked towards the school gates joking and laughing. They always had a cheeky smile on their face, always looking for a 'carry on'.

Although Fela was one of the tallest boys in the school, and the only African in the group, for some reason around his friends he seemed to slink into the background. As soon as they passed the school gate, Uzor approached Fela.

'See you later, Fela,' said his friends, as they headed up the street.

'You awright?' said Uzor.

'I'm good yeah. How about you?' said Fela.

'No bad.'

They continued their small talk and awkward pauses until Fela mentioned that he would be attending a party that weekend.

'Uft, a wis invited tae,' said Uzor.

They chose to meet at Uzor's house and make their way to the party together. This was Uzor's first 'high-school' party, so he made sure he wore his best clothes and got a brand-new haircut, sporting the Will Smith high-top fade, a hairstyle popular with many African boys at the time. However, it wasn't professionally cut and both sides of his hair poked out awkwardly. It was obvious his mother had cut his hair.

He made sure he wore the trainers his Uncle Segun bought him, even though they were now falling apart, with jeans and a varsity jacket from Primark. Uzor gave Fela a call to know his location as they were now late for the party. 'I'm just walking down,' said Fela calmly.

Fela knocks on the door and Uzor lets him in. He is immediately shocked to see what Fela was wearing. Fela wore a strange mix of clothes: a boxy white-and-dark-blue-striped polo with a white underside collar matched with baggy jeans. The shoes he wore weren't Nike, Adidas or designer, but shoes taken from a couple of centuries earlier. Uzor started throwing slight jabs at Fela's shoes, trying to point out what was to become of Fela at the party.

'I like the shoes – very classy,' said Uzor's mother, trying to make Fela feel more comfortable. Fela's shoes had been normal when she was a teenager. Uzor's mother came from a different culture and was rather naive about how things worked in their neighbourhood. Uzor and Fela went to the party which was in the roughest part of the neighbourhood. They found the flat and were surprised to see many senior girls from their school, some of them from Uzor's year. They wore tight-fitting dresses and always seemed to have a cup of alcohol in their hand mixed with something fizzy. Some would deliberately behave as if they were drunk while others were really tipsy. The atmosphere was different from what Uzor was used to and he started to feel popular for the first time, and part of the crowd.

Two other African boys were at the party and they oddly looked familiar to him. One of them wore a bucket hat and vintage clothing and looked very nineties.

He chilled at the side of the living room, sitting on the couch. The other boy danced in the middle of the room to various hip-hop songs. He was a great dancer. Uzor didn't know what to do. After all, this was his first high-school party. He stayed in the kitchen eating the various savoury snacks laid out on the kitchen tables and avoided alcohol. He liked having control over his actions, even if that made him boring to onlookers. He chose to talk to the host of the party, Shiela. She was a tall, muscular girl with a great singing voice and a thick Glaswegian accent. Both Fela and Sheila were in the same year. She loved misleading guys and flirting with them. Fela was an easy target for her as she knew he loved to be validated. After a brief flirting session with Fela, she left him and began talking behind his back, insulting his shoe choice. All the girls erupted in quiet laughter and Fela wondered why.

Uzor decided to come out of his shell and talk to one of the African boys who was dancing in the living room. They looked Uzor up and down sceptically. The dancer soon introduced himself.

'Aight, G? I'm Michael and that's Simon.'

Suddenly, a loud knock came from the front door, which was opened to a group of African boys. Some sported a baldy while others wore short dreadlocks and high-fade haircuts. They all wore trendy clothing and walked with dramatic confidence.

Sheila ran to hug every one of them. She changed the music to hip-hop music immediately pushing the boys into the middle of the living room away from any furniture. Every time the beat reached its highest point, the boys shouted 'Yaaa' and did various popular dances of the time. They created a circle with one boy in the middle performing different dances. Uzor had never seen anything quite like this and he couldn't help but get involved. He jumped into the middle and everyone started shouting as he tried to replicate the Nae Nae dance. He didn't perform it well, but it didn't matter – it was all about having fun.

Uzor, now sweating, left the dancefloor and got acquainted with Simon. Simon was difficult to talk to, as he was very reserved. Uzor took a liking to Simon, admiring his sense of style and laid-back vibe. Simon soon left the party leaving Michael. Uzor ran out of the apartment, after Simon, wondering why he was leaving so early.

'I have to get something man,' said Simon.

Understanding Simon's private nature, Uzor did not ask any more questions and headed back into the party. As he walked in, he was astonished to see Fela behaving like a madman. His body language was overly animated and he started to jump around and lie on the ground at the party. Fela had drunk a small amount of vodka and quickly became the laughingstock of the party. Uzor tried to apprehend his friend, but he refused to listen.

Fela became bold and started talking to various people at the party, including the group of boys, but their respect for him quickly disappeared when they saw his shoes.

Uzor started to distance himself and left the party Fela. Fela however, did not mind. It was as if the lack of parental guidance, authority figures and the abundance of alcohol had let his animal side loose in a frenzy of madness. Uzor tried to shake the feeling that what he saw could have been the real Fela. The night quickly passed and Uzor's first highschool party experience was now over. As he said: 'It was no different from the movies.'

After school on Monday Uzor and Fela walked home together. Uzor refrained from bringing up Fela's behaviour at the party. He wanted to be civil. As they began to walk along the street from the school gates Uzor noticed that Fela seemed uncomfortable, and then began to cough, spitting out large volumes of mucus.

'Are you awright?' said Uzor, his face squeezing in disgust.

His concern for Fela grew as the coughing continued. Fela waved it off as nothing and urged Uzor to continue walking. They stopped at Uzor's favourite neighbourhood bakery to buy some roll and bacon. Fela waited outside and continued to cough out volumes of mucus onto the icy grass. Many thoughts ran through Uzor's mind. This was the first time he had seen Fela like this. Did he have a cold, or had he eaten something bad at lunch?

The baker handed him his roll tucked into a nice white package. Uzor gave the baker £1.50, further dwindling his lunch money for the week.

Uzor and Fela in their impatience decided to take a bus. The bus stop had no shelter and behind the boys was a poorly built 'close' with rotten wood. A 'close' was the slang name for a council apartment. Uzor looked at Fela, who seemed restless, and was scrolling through his phone mindlessly. Uzor didn't know what to ask.

'I forgot something. I need to head,' said Fela.

He crossed the road and headed down the road towards the bakery. Uzor was confused.

'What did you forget?' said Uzor.

Uzor's question was met with silence. It was not until Fela was close to the bakery that he said goodbye.

'I'll see you tomorrow,' said Fela.

Uzor accepted the situation but his curiosity did not. It was not until the next day during school that Uzor was met with the shocking news from Sheila.

'Fela smokes weed,' said Sheila.

Her happiness contrasted with Uzor's disbelief.

Uzor feigned disinterest in Sheila words only for them to be confirmed after school, when he overheard Fela's group of friends talking about meeting each other at their gaffs for some 'ganja'. It was at this point Uzor knew something was wrong. Fela's grades also began to deteriorate. The former smart kid was now becoming a vagabond. Uzor couldn't understand why.

Chapter 12

Prelims

Uzor again began distancing himself from Fela, opting to spend most of his school time sitting at the canteen tables. He also stopped going out for lunch. The only classes Uzor was doing well in were English and Art. His performance in those classes was mediocre but a bit better than most of the students. At this time, his first prelims were coming around. The first prelim always felt like a real exam, even though it did not count towards the final grade. Some of the girls burst into tears, as their anxiety overwhelmed them, whereas other students didn't bother to come in for them.

It was time for Uzor's art prelim. After being told to study during Christmas, he went into the exam with a simple plan: 'I'll just wing it'. After all, it was his first time.

Surprisingly when the marks came back Uzor was ecstatic to find that he had passed and got an incredibly good score.

Doing well in his art prelim made him want to pay extra attention in school, as he was greatly motivated by his art teacher's words. She praised him for his good work and said that his mark had even surprised her. This was new for Uzor as his art teacher was a strange woman. She began every class with a long talk on things entirely opposite to academic stuff. The talks would usually be connected to subjects such as her personal life and the occult. Most students half-listened to her and never took the class seriously. They were always excited to go to art because they knew they could spend two hours doing nothing productive. That year, Uzor's art teacher was retiring and was visibly tired of her job. On her last day, Uzor and James packed up their jotters from English and went up to the art department to say their goodbyes to her. The art teacher was with Uzor's English teacher. Surprised and touched, she smiled at them and said, 'Thank you'.

Chapter 13

Extended Family

The school year was over and summer rolled in. Near the end of summer everyone received their SQA results. Uzor failed Art. At first, he could not believe it and flicked repeatedly through the SQA papers until it dawned on him that he had failed. This unsettled him deeply and Uzor began to question his artistic abilities; a feeling which was further enhanced by an empty summer. The visit to Segun's home didn't feel the same. Segun bought Uzor another pair of shoes, and this time they were Nike Blazers. Uzor did not spend much time drawing and spent most of his time in his house, watching anime and cartoons on his phone.

This all changed when a family member from Nigeria knocked on his front door. In a burst of excitement he opened the door to his mother's second cousin, Tosin, and her husband, Jonathan. They came without their children, Uzor's third cousins.

Uzor felt a deep connection to them and spent a long time with them asking many questions about Nigeria and their family back home. Tosin had a strong Yoruba accent and spoke in pidgin.

'You a aw grown up now,' said Tosin with a sparkle in her eye

That night Uzor's mother received a call from Nigeria. Uzor's first cousin had died in hospital. Uzor's mother was in tears, stricken with grief, and Tosin consoled her. The mood of the house was hysterical. Uzor's father and Jonathan maintained their composure as men.

'This one isn't even crying,' said Jonathan with a slight chuckle, noting Uzor's lack of tears.

Uzor knew what had happened and the gravity of the situation but deep down he just could not feel any emotion. Death was an unfamiliar thing to him. Uzor had not seen his first cousin in years and he felt that he had lost any connections to them. These feelings confirmed his disconnection from his extended family. Uzor's parents had regular prayers in the morning and Uzor was asked to pray. He prayed for longevity. Tosin and Jonathan stayed for an extra week before leaving. Uzor promised to visit them soon.

A week later, summer was over.

Chapter 14

Before And After Exams

Uzor got dressed. He wore his Nikes and had his hair cut professionally by an experienced barber. Uzor was learning. Uzor arrived at school to find the boys in his class excited to be back, some even shouting Uzor's name. The first period was Art and Uzor was stunned to see that all his classmates had also failed. Only one girl scraped a pass. She got a 'D'. She was incredibly good at art and the mark did not reflect her skill one bit. Rumours started to spread that due to the art teacher retiring, she had not bothered to send their artwork to the SQA, leading to the whole class's failure. This greatly angered Uzor and he thought of abandoning art, but after some tough deliberation he decided he would retake it and this time he would pass.

For a few months, the art class had a substitute teacher, an elderly man with hearing defects. He soon left and a new teacher arrived. She was a blonde, beautiful lady and she had a determined look in her eye. She looked battle-ready. Her fervent desire to improve and teach her students greatly inspired them, especially Uzor.

Some of the female students disliked her and she knew, but she continued as before, knowing they would reap the benefits at the end of the year.

The year zipped by and the exam period approached. Uzor began studying for his various classes. Due to his school being in a rough area they weren't as well taught as other secondary schools, as they weren't clear on how the SQA marked the papers. This was because of the change in the exam and marking system going from Intermediates to Nationals. Most of the students whose parents could not afford private tutors had to wing it on exam day. Owing to the high failure rate, many of the teachers gave up on their students, demotivating the further.

Exams were now the talk of the year and took place mostly in May. Uzor's birthday was also approaching and he wanted to have a birthday party, as Sheila's birthday party had inspired him. He was turning 16 years and wanted to have a sixteenth birthday party similar to the Sweet Sixteen shows he'd watched on MTV as a child. He decided to do it the old-fashioned way by writing personal letters of invitations to his classmates. People usually created a Facebook event page inviting other people, but Uzor's last party had been back in his toddler years. He was not savvy about the modern way to invite people to parties and those toddler parties had been planned by his parents. This was the first time he was doing it himself.

Uzor wrote a handful of letters, choosing to give the invitations out before the English exam. All his classmates would be there. Uzor was confident that many of them would attend.

He walked into the canteen at school and looked at Sarah who had now grown up to be a beautiful, gingered-hair girl. Her abundance of freckles was still evident. By this point Uzor and Sarah had patched up their differences. He gave her her invitation first.

'You're invited to ma burfday party,' he said Uzor in his Glaswegian accent.

She received it with a smile and continued to swipe her phone screen.

Uzor made his way around everybody. Everyone looked at the invitation with a confused face, not nearly as happy as Uzor thought they would be.

Maybe it was the wrong time to give it to them, Uzor thought.

Some of them accepted the invitation, whereas others asked where the party was.

The rest were excited to be invited.

The exam period could be regarded as the most nerve-wracking days for any student. It was a cold morning and under the harsh weather Uzor's fingers froze up. You could feel the nervousness in the air. Some of the students feigned their nervousness, but pretending to be hyperactive and talking too much.

Others talked about how they were going to fail, whereas some said they never studied and then laughed. Others again said that they hadn't studied, knowing well that they had spent several months and hours revising for this day.

A teacher called the students and it would be time to go to the exam room. The walk to the room was filled with constant chatter. Others walked silently trying not to lose composure. Some began shouting to get rid of their nerves. As they entered the room, they were told to empty their pockets, turn off their phones and put all their belongings to the side of the room. Any phone which rang would lead to the automatic failing of its owner. Some kids secretly wrote information on their hands or on a note, whereas some of the girls wrote their exam notes on their thighs under their skirts.

Uzor wouldn't cheat. To him it was a waste of time to study if you were going to carry notes to cheat. His hands were still frozen from the weather. He knew he would have to write as fast as he could, as time flew in the exam room. There was always one student who left far too early, with either a smile on their face or a frown. Uzor wrote as much as he could at a speed that slowly warmed his fingers. This allowed him to write efficiently. The exam invigilators walked around checking the students. This time nobody was caught. The exam finished. Uzor made sure he'd written his name and prayed for the best.

The students left the exam room greatly liberated, and began swapping answers, hoping they had written the same thing as everyone else. Uzor also joined in the conversation. Whenever an answer was contrary to what Uzor had written, he felt his confidence dwindle. He separated from his pessimistic classmates and left school. Some of the students stayed, waiting for their next exam. Uzor had no more exams and went home, feeling his body lift as a weight came off his shoulders. He headed to McDonald's for a cheeseburger and medium fries to celebrate.

Chapter 15

Uzor's Birthday Party

Summer approached once again. Uzor had kept in touch with the group of African boys that had been at Sheila's 16th and had invited them to his party. He was excited. His mother assisted him in providing a DJ and the food. On his birthday his father bought Uzor a pair of Adidas Superstars, the trendiest trainers at the time, and his mother gave him some nice shirts from H&M. This was an upgrade from former birthdays. Life started to improve and Uzor made sure he had the best outfit for his party. Since his bad choice of outfit for Sheila's party, he had spent some of his time observing stylish celebrities and trying to replicate their outfits, which had greatly improved his sense of style and colour, and given him confidence in his clothing choices.

He started attending different barber shops and his uncle Segun introduced him to a barbershop in the city centre owned by Ethiopians, who were great hair specialists.

At the front of the shop was a hair salon and nail parlour, while at the back of the shop, was the barbers. The interior was welcoming and fancy. Even the seats were a joy to sit on. Uzor built a relationship with his barber, giving them tips if they did an extremely good job on his hair, or if he was in a good mood. It was always good to tip your barber. It was £10 for a haircut, a great deal for Uzor. He walked out of the barbershop feeling like a new man. That weekend was his birthday party. He was nervous: 'What if nobody turns up or only two people arrive?'

The latter would have been more embarrassing than the former. The first one he could keep quiet about, whereas the second scenario would have two witnesses. His nervousness conflicted with his excitement. The party space was like an office. The DJ was a fair-skinned man with dark eyelashes – it looked like he had mascara on. Uzor quickly got along with him. While at the toilets taking a phone call the DJ walked in with flattery.

The time for the party was approaching. Next to the DJ at the back of the room was a table filled with different flavoured Subway sandwiches and drinks. Suddenly, the doorbell rang. He went to pick up the call and looked at the security camera to see who it was, then quickly ran down stairs and opened the door excited to see the first person to attend his party; a girl from his year, who he had not expected to come. Fela soon arrived with his school friends. They all had apple sours and dragon soup, hiding them from Uzor's mother.

The DJ put on the Cha-Cha Slide and everyone got to the dance floor. This was Uzor's favourite dance song. He was a pro at it and tried to be as smooth as possible during each transition. The energy was rising, but it soon became stale. Uzor looked around and noticed that only two of his classmates turned up. Not wanting to overthink tisand ruin his mood and day he began talking to the people who came to his party.

Uzor was soon approached by his mother. 'It's your friends,' she said.

The group of boys from Sheila's party had turned up. Their leader, Stephan, dapped up Uzor awkwardly and they began dancing, immediately raising the tension and excitement. The girls in the group sat on the seats at the side of the room. Uzor urged them to get up and get involved, even sitting on one of their laps. Stephan and his friends started dancing in the middle of the room, with Stephan showing off his Congolese dancing skills. Everyone went wild.

'Big up my brother right there,' said the DJ.

Uzor was shocked that the DJ was Stephan's brother. Stephan raised his hands leading everyone to cheer. The party was soon reaching its conclusion. Stephan and Uzor rapped to their favourite song together. Stephan rapidly kissed Uzor on the cheek out of excitement in a comic way.

'Good party, bro!' he said completely out of breath. 'When's the next one?'

'Next month we should have one,' lied Uzor, seeing this as an opportunity to get closer to Stephan and his African friends.

'Nicely, bro. You should come out this weekend. Come meet the squad,' said Stephan

His friends repeated the same thing.

When Stephan left, the party also ended.

Uzor's first party experience was great. He received various gifts, money and cards for his birthday and made new African friends. The weekend blazed in and Uzor was on his way to the East End of Glasgow to meet Stephan.

Chapter 16

Africa In Scotland

Uzor got on the number 61 bus to the city centre. Glasgow's summer weather was bipolar: hit or miss. You needed to carry a jacket as a safety precaution. The city centre was packed with many making their way into shopping centres, restaurants, parks and museums. Uzor walked up Buchanan Street, easily the most packed street on a Saturday afternoon during the summer. The best way to manoeuvre was to be as quick as possible. Despite the weather the outdoor cafes were open with rain shelters. Uzor always wondered what the cafes' food was like. He took a quick turn from New Look and made it to the bus stop near Queen Street and got on the bus to the East End and decided to message Stephan to figure out where the area was.

Stephan sent a message: Yo, Uzor, I'll be waiting at the bus stop. Get off that one.

Uzor took heed of the message and kept his eyes out. He didn't have the latest phone so he couldn't access Google Maps.

The trip to the East End was long and revealed to Uzor other rough parts of Glasgow and the nice areas along the way too. There were plenty of open green spaces. Glasgow was not called the greenest city in Europe for no reason. Uzor kept his eyes open taking quick glances at his phone and out of the window. Nearly half an hour had passed and Uzor was growing impatient. The uncomfortable seats were not making it easier for him. The bus Uzor had taken was not a modern FirstBus and had the old dark purple bus handles and seats. He could see engravings of people's gang names on the backs of the seats or phrases stating this and that person fancied each other. Uzor started to feel anxious and tried to message Stephan again but then he glanced out of the window and saw Stephan several metres away at the next bus stop. Uzor quickly pressed the 'stop' button and ran downstairs.

'Cheers,' said Uzor to the bus driver.

Glaswegians were always known to thank their bus drivers for the journey. Doing it was a tradition. Uzor got off the bus and upon seeing Stephan, awkwardly dapped him up. Stephan shook off the awkwardness and led Uzor straight to his place.

'What you sayin, Uzor?' said Stephan.

'I'm good, bro. How about you?' said Uzor, immediately changing his accent.

'Nice, bro. That party last week was mad, bro,' said Stephan.

The area Stephan lived in had a mix of middle-class homes and flats. It was fairly clean but each house was so similar that you could spend hours walking in circles. Stephan took Uzor through a shortcut leading them up several hills and then sneaked through a few ripped fences. Uzor looked around seeing many children in their primary school uniform walking with their siblings and parents. They finally made it to the school and waited for Stephan's sister. The school bell rang and Stephan's sister, Joana, emerged from the school line.

Stephan's sister looked old enough to be in her first year of secondary. She had a stern look that revealed a strong attitude. She gave Uzor a glare and twitched her lips. As soon as she looked at Stephan, her face lit up. She was evidently fond of her brother. Stephan did not bother to ask her how her day was. His full intention was on heading home.

The walk back was faster. Stephan walked straight into the living room while his sister went straight to the kitchen where their mother was and began telling her mother about her day at school.

The living room was dark and had two black couch-es with a large flat-screen television placed on top of a dark=brown varnished sideboard. There were two figures sitting on the individual couches. The dimness of the room made it difficult for Uzor to see who they were. They both get up and approach Uzor.

'What's good, bro?' said Simon.

'Uft! Simon. I didn't know you knew these two, Stephan,' said Uzor.

'Reunion, bro,' said Stephan.

Michael and Simon dapped Uzor awkwardly. They all took their seats and Stephan began joking around with Michael and Simon. Their spat continued while Uzor watched them, laughing. During all this, it became clear that Stephan was very popular in the African community in Glasgow and Uzor knew being close to him would bring him closer to people who were just like him. In this way he was certain that he would no longer experience racism and loneliness.

The boys left the house and headed to the convenience store, where the boys bought various snacks and made their way around the area. Michael and Simon lived in the same area as Stephan.

'Would you shag a granny?' said Michael.

Uzor was silent for a while causing both Simon and   Michael to look at Uzor sideways.

Why is he spending so much time thinking about that? thought Michael.

A few more seconds passed.

'No, I wouldn't,' said Uzor.

It was an odd question but sometimes boys say strange things. They soon got to Simon's flat and made their way upstairs. They waited outside Simon's door.

'If I don't come out in 10 minutes that means I have to stay in,' said Simon.

15 minutes passed, and they took that as a sign. They left the flat and headed to Michael's flat. He lived just around the corner. The iron railings on the outside steps were pink and rusty like at Uzor's flat. They walked into Michael's flat. He had a few brothers who poked their heads around the corner. One of them had a wandering look, like he was observing Uzor. Neither of Michael's parents was in and he headed straight to his room, which was incredibly small. It felt full with just the three of them. Michael put on his PlayStation 2 and started playing NBA 2K. Remembering his bad history with consoles, Uzor declined a shot, preferring to watch. Uzor noticed Michael had speakers and tried to turn them on, but to no avail.

'They're broken,' said Michael.

Time passed and Stephan had to make his way home. Michael couldn't come along due to him having to take care of his brothers. Stephan daps up Michael - that is how they say 'see you later' - and makes his way back home with Uzor. When they got home, Stephan and Uzor went upstairs into the toilet. Stephan locks the door. Uzor wondered why they were in the toilet, but Stephan never said a word. The toilet looked unkempt, had rust, and mould growing at different corners. Stephan pulls out a grinder and a green pouch from his pocket. He lays them on top of the toilet tank. He sprinkled the green leaves into the grinder, covered it with the lid and twisted it a few times before spending time rolling it into a joint.

After a few failed attempts he finally made the correct roll and he put it into his pockets. Uzor
watched in shock but put on a mask to cover his
true feelings. He could not believe what he was
seeing. This shockingly changed his view of
Stephan. Stephan smiled at him unaware of Uzor's
dislike of drugs. They went downstairs and went out
back where Stephan could not be seen by his
mother. The sun reared its head and began to bite
their skin. Stephan began to smoke his joint. He
offered Uzor some but Uzor politely refused. Uzor
was naive to Stephan's true character and wasn't
sure on what he was getting into. Does he avoid
Stephan and go back to being alone? Uzor didn't
know what to do. He thought maybe not everyone
was like him and that nobody is perfect. Maybe he
should just become friends with him and ignore his
bad faults. Maybe he should just...

It was soon time for Uzor to head back home.
They waited at the bus stop.

There was an awkward silence that lingered in
the air. It was as if they were both hiding something
from each other.

Stephan decides to break the silence.

'Bro, come meet the squad in town this weekend!'

Uzor accepted the invitation. He just wanted to
have African friends and people he could relate to.

He didn't fit in at school or in his neighbourhood and the only time he felt closer to home was when he was around his black friends, especially ones who weren't too influenced by Scottish culture like Fela. The sun went down, and the grey clouds began to cover the sky as Uzor's bus slowly drove towards the bus stop.

Chapter 17

Meeting His African Brothers

Uzor made his way down Argyle Street. Glasgow City Centre was packed. The men wore head and t-shirts while females had unearthed the denim shorts and sundresses that had been packed away for months. This was a rare sight in Glasgow. Buskers took their place at the side of the street and the street performers stood in the middle drawing crowds. One of them was surrounded by pigeons and seemed to be feeding them seed. Pigeon-feeding always reminded Uzor of the homeless lady in Home Alone 2. Another street performer was blowing bubbles and many children congregated around them with their parents. There was also an elderly man who danced and wore white gloves on his hands, which had various colours on the fingertips. His dancing sometimes looked like he was fighting an imaginary opponent.

The walk to St Enoch's Shopping Centre passed various bus stops and cars going down one-way streets.

The mix of people talking and the vehicles made the streets noisy. However, no one was aware of the amplified sound; it was like white noise to them. The aroma of smoke and gas filled the air and Uzor's nostrils. He reached the front entrance of St Enoch's shopping centre. A couple of tall, double-glazed glass doors with vertical steel handles controlled the influx of people coming in and out. Uzor had to wait several seconds before he could get in.

The shopping centre was fairly new to him. He remembered at primary school he had sung Christmas carols with the school choir in St Enoch's Shopping Centre, but he had never gone around the place himself.

The first thing Uzor noticed was the security guard and charity stand to the right of him. St Enoch's had three floors. The ground floor Uzor had two routes. The right side led you to the various shops on the ground floor. The left side had escalators that led up to the second floor. He walked to the left side of St Enoch towards the escalators. While on the escalators he looked to his right. Parallel to the escalator, heading back down to the ground floor, was a vast window that overlooked St Enoch SPT Subway Station glass canopy and The Bank of Scotland building. Near the top of the escalators at his left was a fancy restaurant with a turquoise glass interior. It looked exclusive, hovering as if it was separate from the rest of the building. Uzor got off the escalators and passed by people strolling towards the escalators leading to the ground floor.

Uzor looked up and saw a set of escalators in the middle of the floor that led to the toy store Hamleys. The vivid crimson design caught his eye and he hoped to walk in there someday. Uzor made his way through St Enoch's passing a few shops before entering the food court.

Instantly the volume increased, assaulting Uzor's eardrums. The court was filled with many families and friends eating fast food provided by different fast-food restaurants. At his right was McDonald's was opposite the stairs to the third floor. Uzor went upstairs and took his seat, wondering where Stephan and his friends were.

Uzor pulled out his phone, swiped left and right, and messaged Stephan: 'Where are yous?'

Uzor waited for a reply. To pass the time, he looked around the third floor and observed the people there. There was a balcony that looked over the second-floor food court and a wide window at his right, far in the background that overlooked St Enoch Square. There was a children's soft play near the third floor's toilets. Uzor would watch as the children would express their innate enthusiasm or cry if they got hurt. The sun rays began to beat off the white kaleidoscope-like structure on the ceilings and red chairs creating a dazzling but calming feeling inside St Enoch's. Fifteen minutes passed and Uzor became impatient. He pulled out his phone to message Stephan again when suddenly a message appeared: 'We're coming up now, bro.'

Uzor shook his head. He'd forgotten that Africans were notorious for being late for almost everything but court appearances and were so bad that the term 'African Time' had been created to excuse their laziness and lack of punctuality. Of course, not all Africans were late to events but it was so prevalent in their community that the term had stuck. Uzor stood up and had decided to take a walk to Hamleys when Stephan came into view with two of the boys who had attended Uzor's party, who looked European or Middle Eastern.

'Bro, yous are late,' said Uzor.

'Sorry, bro, we had some things we had to sort out,' said Stephan, giving the two boys a knowing look.

'Ah, alright, bro,' said Uzor.

'Bro, that party you had was mad. Where's the invite for the next one?' said Jasser.

'Yeah, bro. It was lit!' said Alberto.

Stephan introduced both of his friends. They were both standing behind him. Jasser was an average height boy. He wore a snapback, jeans, and a jumper, while Alberto, the one on the left of Jasser was slightly shorter and wore a shabby tracksuit and a pair of Adidas running shoes. They both approached Uzor to dap him. Uzor managed to do the handshake fairly well. He had practised countless times by himself and in his head since his time at Stephan's house. Uzor thought about having another party and wondered if Stephan wouldn't want to hang around with him if he didn't.

'Bro, let's go KFC. Everyone's there, yar,' said Stephan.

Uzor trailed behind them. They went down the stairs, left St Enoch's and crossed the road towards the 'Four Corners KFC', so-called because the junction had two major fast-food restaurants, McDonald's and KFC. As they walked into KFC and immediately the mood of the place overwhelmed Uzor. There were so many Africans in one space that they eclipsed other nationalities and races. Stephan was the obvious leader as everyone walked towards him. Uzor was ecstatic to be with, as he would say, 'his kind of people'. This was the reverse of what he had experienced in the past. He no longer had to lie to his school friends that he had 'black friends" outside school. Stephan was socially intelligent and charismatic. Everything he did was guaranteed to muster intrigue and reverence. Everyone loved him. The girls whose laps Uzor had sat on at his party approached him.

'Hi. I like your style. Nice Superstars,' said one of the girls.

Uzor had made sure he'd worn his best clothes, and had used his birthday money to buy an Adidas jacket and cap. The effort seemed to be paying off.

Uzor was then approached by boys who had also been at his party

'Bro, are you Nigerian?' one asked.

All of a sudden Uzor became the centre of attention.

Pride, a Congolese boy and the tallest in the group, approached Uzor, dapped him up and asked him to record a video of himself and his boys rapping to a song.

Is this a test? Uzor thought as he took the phone and began recording, placing his own phone beside it to upload the video on his SnapChat. While recording the boys rapping, he began to notice their style. They all wore similar clothes – Adidas, Nike – and talked in slang he couldn't interpret, like they were speaking another language. They moved around like they owned KFC, laughing and having a good time. The group exuded a strong collective spirit, infecting anyone who came close to them, including Uzor. After recording the boys, Uzor was approached by a different girl, Gemma, who knew Uzor from the party.

'Uzor, are you in the groupchat?' she asked.

'No,' said Uzor.

Gemma pulled out her phone and began showing Uzor the groupchat, which had more than fifty members and was growing. As soon as Uzor was added he saw it as a sign that he was now a member of the group. Deep down all that was running through his head was, 'At last – friends who accept me.'

Uzor continued his chat with different members of the group and tried his best to bring out his extroverted side. The group saw Uzor as quite charming and enjoyed his company.

By this time. Stephan had left KFC with another group of boys, whose demeanour was rather intimidating. You could tell they didn't like prolonged eye contact. As soon as Stephan left, the energy of the group declined. Stephan's motive for leaving was unknown to Uzor. He wanted to follow Stephan but his eyes were locked on a light-skinned girl in the group, with a large afro, half of which was hidden by her beanie. She wore tight jeans that revealed her curves and a white t-shirt with cute graphics on them. What really drew her to Uzor was her light brown eyes and her innocent elegant foreign accent.

'What's her name?' Uzor asked Pride.

'That's Frida,' Pride said. 'You want her, bro? Let me introduce you.'

At first this offer from Pride made Uzor nervous. However, it was what he secretly wanted. Frida went outside KFC and waited at the front. Pride and Uzor followed. They approached Frida who was surrounded by different members of the group. Pride began talking to Frida, their speech inaudible, due to everything going around them. Uzor grew some courage. He was on an emotional high and he had never felt so social before. It was as if he had drunk alcohol. He approached Frida and with a cool demeanour muttered, 'What's your number? Just in case ... for future parties.'

Frida made no reaction but gave Uzor her number and took his.

With that, the day ended.

Uzor felt the group was growing on him. He liked their camaraderie and the way they seemed like a family. Uzor got on the evening bus home. He had never been this late home before. As soon as he got home his mother noticed Uzor's face was beaming.

'What time is this?' his mother asked.

'I met all these African people my age!' said Uzor as he began to describe his day.

He then went into his room and began typing into the groupchat.

'Yo, there's a few parties this weekend, broo. Who's coming?' messaged Jesser.

Many added that they were going, including Uzor – his first party with the group. Uzor did not know what to expect.

'Can I bring three people?' someone messaged in the chat.

'Yeah, bring as many people as you can,' Jesser replied.

Uzor decided to contact Fela to invite him to the party. He secretly enjoyed Fela's presence at parties and saw this as a way for Fela to avoid the rough neighbourhood. The next day when sitting in the back row next to the church entrance. Uzor received a text from Frida: 'Hi.'

Surprised at how easy Frida was making it for him, he decided to take a chance and continue texting her.

They planned to meet on Wednesday, a few days before the party, to watch a film together. Wednesday flew in and Uzor waited outside St Enoch's waiting for Frida to go on their first date together.

Chapter 18

First Date

Frida approached Uzor. Her outfit was similar to the one she'd been wearing when Uzor first met her. The only difference was that she was not sporting a beanie, which made her puffy afro glisten in the sun. Uzor felt prepared. He had spent most of his time before the date googling, 'How to survive your first date?' and 'What to say on your first date?' From what he read, girls like confident guys, so he displayed a cocky and confident persona to impress her. Frida did not take notice of Uzor's posturing. She was very timid and was not fluent in English so getting a smooth conversation from her was difficult.

They walked to Cineworld. They start their journey by walking up Buchanan Street. The streets were empty today. 12-1PM in Glasgow City Centre was usually scarce with people. This made it easier to navigate the streets. They got to the top of Buchanan Street and took a turn from John Lewis to enter Renfrew street.

This held Cineworld. Before they got their tickets, they entered Poundland along Sauchiehall Street to buy cheap snacks. The snacks included Haribo's, crisps and toffee popcorn. Poundland was their best option because cinema food was expensive. They pay for their food at Poundlands counter and make their way to the Cineworld lobby. The lobby was dark but the bright-red and light blue lights gave the room a dynamic appearance. The open space allowed you to forget your worries. Uzor and Frida both walk up to the movie selection. Frida was excited to watch Jurassic Park, but Uzor wanted to watch a different movie. Not wanting to upset her, he capitulated. At the ticket booth, Uzor and Frida had planned to both buy discounted tickets with their Young Scot cards, but Frida had forgotten to bring hers, so Uzor felt compelled to pay for the rest of her ticket.

They made their way up the escalators refusing to talk to each other on their way to the floor, where Uzor's hunger urged him to buy a hotdog and a large popcorn from the food counter even though he had already bought food from Poundland. Any food that was not from Cineworld was not allowed into the cinema, but knowing this ahead Uzor and Frida both carried backpacks hiding food from staff.

'Screen 2 on your left,' said the usher.

The film was just starting. The sound as they made their way inside slowly drowned out. There was something suspenseful about the walk to the screen.

The darkness, screen lights beaming on the seats and the crowd of people shrouded in black staring at you as you walked out of the corner to head up their stairs and find your seats. Frida wanted to sit far back so Uzor followed her. They took their seats but before they could become fully comfortable, a couple quietly insisted that Uzor and Frida were sitting in their seats. Uzor moved along two seats but they were once again told to move as another couple arrived to take their seats. However, before the movie started, Uzor and Frida had finally gotten two empty spaces directly in the middle of the back row.

During the countless adverts, Uzor contemplated putting his arm around Frida as he had seen in several romance movies. The film started and the room became darker. Couples around them began to warm up to each other putting heads on shoulders. Uzor then saw this as a sign for him to act. He put his arm around Frida and as the movie progressed, they began holding hands. Frida got scared at certain scenes and squeezed Uzor's hand for assurance. The movie was reaching its climax and a romance scene came in. The scene reminded Uzor that he had not kissed her. He just had to do it. His body became tense and his stomach began to leap the more he thought about it. Then in a spark, Uzor leaned over to kiss Frida. His body relaxed into it and became warm. There was something life-giving about a kiss especially to someone you were attracted to. He was excited everywhere, including down there.

'I have to meet my friend after this,' Frida said.

Uzor and Frida got up and left Screen 2. Uzor wanted to meet Frida's friend and went with her. They walked back down Buchanan Street holding hands. Uzor felt brazen, took out his phone and began recording himself and Frida. He smiled at the camera while Frida shyly covered her face. He could not figure out why she was covering her face and thought that Frida possibly did not want to be seen with him. However, Frida was just shy and did not mean any harm. They made their way to the Four Corners McDonalds' where Frida spotted her friend.

'Lisa!' she shouted Frida

This was the first time Uzor had seen Frida so ecstatic. She began speaking in Portuguese. Lisa quickly turned her attention to Uzor.

'Hi, I'm Lisa! Don't take my sister away!' she said Lisa.

Uzor chuckled but he found it rather strange that Lisa would make such a remark. She looked at Uzor with a possessive eye. He couldn't help but think that there was something else behind her facade. Lisa and Frida continued their chat while Uzor ordered a Mcflurry and cheeseburger for himself. He left McDonald's and approached Frida and Lisa. Lisa was taking her leave: 'See you later,' she said.

Uzor felt he had passed the best-friend test and offered his McFlurry to Frida who declined.

Frida had to head home.

They walked to the bus stop and Uzor tried to strike a conversation about the movie but Frida had reverted to her shy and timid ways. The change was like night and day and Uzor could not shake the feeling that he was dealing with the masked Frida rather than the true one. They shared one more kiss before Frida got on her bus marking the end of their first date.

Uzor also made his way home reminiscing on his kiss with Frida and messaging her plenty of times on the bus. They sent each other several love heart emojis after each message and made sure the emojis and 'xs' matched. It became a ritual.

The party was soon approaching. Before the party Uzor went out to visit the group once again, wasting time and doing anything they could to enjoy summer, even going to the temporary amusement park in St Enoch's Square, although he avoided the rides. Uzor didn't enjoy the G-force feeling.

Frida's friends encourage Uzor and Frida's relationship. Some of the boys came and dapped Uzor, wanting to know about his sex life.

'Have you shagged her?' said one of the boys.

Being a virgin in the group was embarrassing.

Even Michael, who was dating Frida's friend and Stephan were noted saying, 'You and Frida, yeah?'

Uzor and Frida soon became the talk of the group and Uzor loved it. The only person who did not mention Frida was Simon.

He was rather reclusive and wasn't curious about Uzor's life unlike the rest of them. He spent much of his time playing basketball and was seen as a loner. Uzor wasn't sure if he was part of the group or not, although he seemed to be highly respected among its members.

Frida's friend Lisa lived in a children's home and often hung around the group to curb her boredom. She asked Uzor about Frida, which made Uzor think she was strange. Lisa could have easily messaged Frida, but she chose to ask Uzor. Was this a test? Uzor maintained his composure and behaved cordially towards Lisa. He noticed that whenever Lisa spoke to him she had a slight sparkle in her eyes and colour in her cheeks. The day before the party, Lisa pulled Frida away from Uzor demanding that she spend time with her. At first this made sense – Frida and Lisa were friends – but Lisa's hostile looks kept Uzor on guard.

Uzor started to know more about Frida's personal life, her family and her inner world. She didn't have a father, so her mother had to work nights to pay the bills. Frida took care of her siblings and the additional chores. Uzor and Frida often got into long phone calls and Uzor enquired after her family as he listened to their voices in the background. She answered all his questions in a stressed tone. In a way Uzor was an escape for Frida.

Uzor was infatuated with Frida but his infatuation blinded him to his future undoing.

Chapter 19

Hedonism

The party day arrived.

'Yo! Everyone meets at St Enoch,' messaged Jasser in the chat.

That evening everyone made their way there and Uzor met Fela at the front of his flat before they got on the early bus to city centre. The streets were empty, cold and the sun was setting. They met with the group at St Enoch and Uzor immediately began to match their frenetic energy. He introduced Fela to them. The boys all huddled around two tables at the food court. Fela went around them all dapping up, getting on easily and quickly with the group. Several of the group members were , as expected, but they were soon on their way to catch the bus 75 to their party destination.

At the bus stop Uzor and Stephan began throwing insults at each other. To outsiders the insults might have seemed antagonizing, but this was just friendly banter to them.

Uzor felt bold and commented on Stephan's smoking habits in front of the whole group.

'That's why your lips are so black,' said Uzor.

Everyone laughed, except Stephan.

The bus arrived. Pride got on first, showed the bus driver an expired ticket, then passed it backwards to another member of the group unbeknownst to the driver. The pattern continued until they were all on the bus. They all headed upstairs and took over half of the bus seats. Uzor and Fela sat next to each other. The energy m was riveting but Uzor suddenly started to feel low. Fela noticed and instead of consoling Uzor, he quickly moved seats, to sit beside Simon. Uzor was offended by what Fela had done but his lack of energy discouraged him from saying anything. Instead, he looked out the window and observed the streets of Glasgow. The bus stopped at ASDA. A couple of his school classmates from fifth year, a year above him, made their way to the top deck One of them, Connie, glared at the group, but then sat at the front. Connie and his boys were quiet for the remaining bus ride and got off before the group. Silence followed them. Uzor was surprised. Connie was known for being a loud-mouthed racist, but the presence of the group had shut him up, which made Uzor feel powerful. The people who had bullied him from secondary school were now intimidated by him.

'We get off here,' said Jasser.

The group rushed downstairs, their presence intimidating everyone as they walked by. They made their way to the gaff, resembling a marching band. Some walked slowly at the back while some were at the front chatting away, talking about how 'wavy' the party would be. Uzor didn't say much on the walk there. He was too tired. The closer they got to the apartment, the stronger the smell of dust and grass was. It felt like some remote part of Glasgow. They passed a few apartments and brushed along brick walls before they reached the front door of the apartment. They were people already there – a group of intimidating-looking boys and some girls dressed in tight-fitting red and white dresses. Stephan walked towards the group of boys. The way everyone looked at them made it clear that they were important. There were four of them and they all wore a scowl on their face, making it clear they were not people to mess with. One of them stood proudly at the front, standing next to the grass hedges. There was something about him that screamed 'leader'.

'Who's that?' asked Uzor.

'That's Toure and that's the C-Boys gang,' said Pride.

Jasser opened the front door to allow everyone into the flat and they made their way upstairs to the designated flat. Uzor pushed closer to the front and nodded at Toure, who in turn nodded back. Uzor then nodded at another member of C-Boys. He was overweight and had a very mean look on his face.

His voice was also high-pitched. He ignored Uzor. In turn, Uzor turned away, deciding not to take it personally.

Uzor slumped on the sofa at the back of the room. Some of the boys smoked out of the window while others put on their beat pills and began playing the latest Meek Mill song. However, this was not enough to get everyone hyped.

'This is a sausage fest ,maan', said one of the boys.

'Sausage fest' was a term to describe a party that had more guys than girls. Many of the guys' sole purpose for coming to parties was to flirt with girls so their absence immediately ruined their motives.

'Bro, you okay?' one of the boys asked Uzor. They noticed Uzor's loss of energy. He was beginning to develop flu-like symptoms.

'Broo, those shoes are mad,' said another boy, who'd noticed Uzor superwhite Adidas trainers. While the boy admired his trainers, all Uzor noticed was that the boy looked too young to be at the party.

People spread themselves around the flat. Wondering where Stephan and Fela were, Uzor got up from his sofa and walked to the corridor. He tried to walk into the room on his left, but it was locked.

'No one is allowed in. The C-Boys are there, including Stephan,' said Pride.

It was hard to ignore the thick smell of marijuana coming from the room.

Uzor walked into the opposite room to see a scattered floor with several mattresses. He could not tell if the room had a bed or not. The room was packed with people and Uzor still could not find Fela.

'Where's Fela?' asked Uzor.

'He went out,' said Gemma, who was very drunk.

The room soon became too claustrophobic for Uzor.

'Let's go take pictures,' said Pride. Uzor followed Pride to the kitchen to take photos for their social media accounts. Although Uzor was extremely tired, he still tried to look as good as possible knowing that the photo would be scrutinised online. After Uzor left the kitchen and saw Fela enter through the front door. His eyes were red and squinty, completed by a smile of temporary ecstasy. Uzor immediately knew what Fela was up to. He did not say anything to him, leaving him to make his own decisions.

As she rested on the mattress two white Scottish men walked in. They both looked like they were in their thirties and it wasn't clear who'd let them in. By their slow movements and overt giddiness, Uzor could tell that they were drunk.

What are these two guys doing at a teenage party? he wondered.

Suddenly, one the girls started shouting, 'LEAVE HER!'

One of the men had touched one of the girls and her friend began defending her vehemently.

The man tried to calm her down, but the friend was having none of it. Her anger animated her facial expressions. Stephan overheard and walked into the room and started to defend the girls, calling them his 'sisters'. Stephan walked out of the room and Uzor noticed how drunk and high he was. Uzor knew things were going to go downhill fast. He just did not know to what extent. He called a taxi, figuring it was time to leave.

'We will have a taxi to you in 30 minutes,' said the taxi company

Uzor knew that 30 minutes was too long to wait before the mayhem kicked off.

Jasser and the boys pressured the men outside the flat. The two men were surrounded by the partygoers. Some stayed upstairs to watch through the window. The daylight had completely gone and the only thing that shone was the light from the windows and flat corridors. The men had their backs to the road. The C-Boys faced the men, revealing their aggressive steely eyes. The tension was palpable.

'Fucking bunch of black bastards!' The two men threw various insults, but the C-Boys did not flinch.

'If you want a scrap, let's scrap,' said one of the C-Boys.

People knew what was going to happen and brought out their phones to press 'record'.

The shortest member of the C-Boys became frantic and started pacing up and down shouting, 'WHERE'S TOURE?'

Adrenaline influenced their behaviour. Toure came down and walked in front of the C-Boys. He raised his chin showing no sign of fear. The two men's faces were red with anger. One of them threw their glass at Toure's face. He dodged and the glass smashed onto the concrete. No one heard the smash as all eyes were on the ensuing fight. Multiple fists were thrown, loud feminine screams were uttered and the scene became blurry. It was like the feeling you get when your life flashes before your eyes and everything becomes blurry. The fight was so rapid that Uzor didn't manage to press record on his phone.

Uzor received a text notifying him of his taxi's arrival and made his way from the flat to meet the taxi on the other side. The boys continued throwing punches. Uzor got into the taxi but kept his eyes glued to what was going on at the flat. The C-Boys were dominating the two men but all that changed when a 6' 7'' muscular man walked out of the flat and walked towards Toure who backed up. Suddenly, Toure swung a punch at the man's face connecting slightly. The taxi started to move. The feeling that he had got involved with the wrong people rose in Uzor, but he still felt that it was not time to leave. The group was like a drug that pulled him back again and again. It wasn't long till Uzor was out again with the group.

Chapter 20

Troon

For the next few days, all the group ranted and raved about was the fight at the party, sharing their videos of the fight alongside laughing and shocked emojis. As the days went on questions about Uzor's promised party also began to pop up and he didn't know what to do. He thought they had completely forgotten but as with every lie, it always comes back to haunt you. Uzor had to continue the lie.

'It's been moved,' said Uzor.

Jasser was anxious for a party and was disappointed at Uzor's answer.

'Bro, there isn't any party, is there?' he said.

Uzor denied Jasser's claim, but by that time Jasser had understood what was really going on.

Uzor thought his position in the group was gone, but by the faces of the members and Jasser he knew that he hadn't needed to lie from the start. They liked him anyway, with or without the party.

The sun brought down its heavy heat once again and everybody had their 'taps aff'; a saying for when the sun was piping hot in Glasgow, referring to the rarity of the sun in Scotland.

'Let's go Trooon,' messaged Jasser in the chat.

'Let's go next week,' messaged Gemma.

'What if we die before that time? Let's go now!' messaged Jasser.

Uzor had never been to the beach without his family before, so this was a first for him and Uzor decided to go that weekday with the group. Frida was babysitting so she couldn't make it. Uzor added Fela to the group chat so he could also come to the beach. When Thursday came round, with help from his mother, Uzor made sure he wore the right attire. He was fairly insecure about his weight so he didn't take shorts with him, opting to wear H&M joggers instead and a white t-shirt, with his Superstars and backpack. Everyone made their way to the city centre. Uzor had never seen so many teenagers in Glasgow before. The only day that could match the scene was Boxing Day, when teenagers from different parts of Glasgow made their way to the city centre to spend their Christmas money. Today was no different.

He met up with the group in Glasgow Central Station and they made their way to the trains that were filled with young people. Other passengers had to squeeze their way through narrow spaces to get off the train. A few metres from Uzor, among the crowd, was a group of girls.

They put their speakers on, blasting Calvin Harris and various Soundcloud house music, and had paint on their faces. You could tell this was going to be serious. Uzor sat at a train table, opposite Pride and his girl, and put on his own HipHop/Trap music. Everyone bopped their heads to the beat, confirming Uzor's great taste in music. The train stopped at Troon and a horde of teenagers got off.

The walk to Troon was legendary. Imagine this: a horde of teenagers all in different shapes and sizes making their way through a quiet town – it was something to marvel at. Uzor noticed the air change: it was clean and silky smooth and the dust from the sand made its way through his nostrils, giving him a strange but therapeutic feeling. They got onto the beach and everyone made their stay. It was not until a second batch of teenagers from the next train made their way to the beach that everyone went crazy. Music blasted from different corners of the beach, and underage girls, all drunk and high, dismissed thirsty men left and right.

Stephan and the C-Boys made their way along the beach with their usual scowl and dominating presence. Uzor took his shoes off, dug his legs into the warm sand and looked up to the sky. Fela and Simon made their way to the sea and Uzor followed. The salty water was refreshing. Uzor even took a quick swim, plunging his whole body into the water. He was a poor swimmer, so he didn't go very far as he was afraid of sharks, even though they're no sharks in Troon.

There was something about swimming in the sea that made a beach experience fulfilling.

When boredom gets into a group of diverse teenagers , violence can crop up and trouble soon ensues. The group made their way back to the train when an argument between a gang in Troon and the C-Boys kicked off. Uzor was walking and talking with Stephan, but as soon as Stephan noticed the argument he shouted, 'What's this? What's this?' and swaggered back towards the C-Boys.

For the first time Uzor saw a break in Stephan's usual friendly demeanour. People say true character shows when someone is angry and Stephan was no different. The overweight C-Boy began to run his mouth to one of the Troon gang members who looked visibly distressed. The C-Boys took their leave, but the Troon gang members followed them.

'Why you following us?' said Toure calmly.

By this point they were all surrounded by youths at the beach. Uzor again began to experience the same feeling he had had at the party. Sound seemed to stop. All he could hear were the waves breaking on the shore. Suddenly, the overweight C-Boy threw a solid jab at the Troon gang member leading all the C-Boys and Stephan to form a circle around him and battering him with passion. Whenever the Troon boy lifted his head his face was volleyed like a football.

Group members who were not part of the C-Boys even joined in.

Big muscular African boys pounded their fists and legs on the boy's face. The boy held his own and did not fall, but his face was swollen and bloody. Soon the authorities made their way to the scene and everyone ran to the train station. The C-Boys blended in with the crowd and disappeared, along with Stephan. Uzor made his way to the station, but then headed back for his backpack. On his way he passed the Troon boy whose eyes were 'bubbling', as he held back his tears in embarrassment but still stood tall.

Uzor's first beach experience without his family was not what he'd expected. He'd expected beach balls and games, not gang fights. The more he got involved with the group, the more they pulled him in deeper into their abyss. After Troon, news outlets began reporting on the horde of teenagers who 'made their way to Troon' and people began calling Uzor's new group of friends the ones who 'Ran Troon beach'.

Again, discussion about the fight at Troon began to circle.

'Who wants to stab you. Stephan?' messaged Uzor.

'The people I stole weed from at Troon,' messaged Stephan.

'Be careful Stephan! Not everyday is gangster,' messaged Uzor.

'I know, bro,' messaged Stephan.

Chapter 21

Drama

A house party was happening the following week and this time Frida was able to attend. They planned to meet each other there. Uzor was becoming quite well known among the group and was seen as their most stylish member. To this party he wore a bandanna and a fancy shirt – the same one he'd worn to his birthday party – and his Superstars. He made sure to polish his trainers before leaving that day. As usual, they all met in the city centre and made their way to the party. Frida arrived slightly late with her friend Lisa and ignored Uzor throughout the party. She swallowed unhealthy percentages of alcohol and stomped around the house like a crazed individual. This was a side of Frida Uzor had never seen before and he wasn't sure what to do.

Uzor grabbed her and carried her upstairs on his shoulders . He tried to get through to her, by expressing his dislike of her behaviour, but she ignored and gave him a look as if he was just another guy.

She began flirting with other men at the party, enraging and belittling Uzor. The C-Boys also attended this party. They came through the back of the house hopping over several wooden fences to get there. They made sure to walk around the party looking at each male at the party to intimidate them. If you held eye contact too long you could be in for trouble. Soon the party giver said that his uncle was making his way back and everyone had to leave the party as he had not told any family member that he was having a party at the house. Everyone quickly left. Uzor waited for Frida, who took her heels off to walk. Uzor looked around. He felt like a vagabond going from one party to the next with no true direction; hedonism at its highest. At the bus stop two conflicting stories were circulating: the first was that the party was still happening; and the second was that it wasn't. Uzor had had enough. He got on the bus along with several others who'd been at the party. They took their seats upstairs and began their wild antics. Some even recorded the scene for their SnapChat. Uzor opened the group chat.

'The party's still going,' someone messaged in the chat. Uzor, not wanting to go home, left the bus along with Fela, Lisa and Frida and waited 30 minutes for the next bus back. Fela sat at the bus stop, pulled out a cigarette and tried to light it. Uzor became angry once again and scolded Fela: 'What are you dane smoking?' he shouted.

Fela's eyes were already red and he looked extremely tired. He didn't answer. They got on the bus but it was the bus to the city centre so they could go home. Uzor had enough. On this bus, Uzor continued to scold Fela, taking out all his frustration on him. Frida sat far from him with Lisa, and looked on with her usual poker face. It was as if she had returned back to normal. Uzor didn't say a word to Frida throughout the bus journey and his journey home. Not one message was shared between them.

The next day was church. Uzor made the decision to break up with Frida. He had contemplated it for a while, but his mind was made up. When Frida saw the message, she answered with laughing emojis and sent voice recordings of Lisa and herself joking about the issue, making it clear that Uzor was not too important to her. Uzor felt liberated. He went out with the group the next day and kissed one of the girls. Pictures and gossip about the kiss spread throughout the group.

'Why would she do that when Uzor broke up with her?' messaged Gemma.

Drama ensued.

Chapter 22

His Voice

Summer was coming to an end and the group slowly began to fizzle out, as many only stayed in the group during the summer. Uzor was once again back at school and was surprised to discover that over the summer his classmates had been watching his antics on social media with the group. Uzor became the talk of the school. Everyone wanted to be around him, and some tried to ridicule him out of envy. However, Uzor's confidence over the summer had risen tremendously. Being associated with a group that was popular made him walk around with a certain air of 'I don't need anyone at this school'. The girls in his year began to warm up to him, stroking his ego

'You actual go to aw these parties, man. Invite iz!' said one of the girls.

At the weekends or after school Uzor would make his way to meet the group and on one of these occasions Uzor laid his eyes on a beautiful mixed-race girl called Selena.

She had a large afro and took a liking to Uzor, calling him, 'the most handsome boy in the group'. Uzor saw this as a chance and started messaging her and they soon started dating. Selena was very beautiful and turned heads wherever she was. She had an elegant and silent charisma.

'You guys are so cute!' said one of the girls. On the outside they looked perfect, but Uzor was too insecure to handle the constant ogling and catcalling of other men. Even members in the group began making passes at her and flirting with her. Selena told Uzor about an incident when he hadn't been around, when Alberto had tried to touch her. Uzor approached Alberto angrily, but Alberto soon apologized. His apology wasn't well received, as Uzor could tell that Alberto wasn't too sorry about what he had done. Before Uzor and Selena started dating Alberto had mentioned how pretty she was and it was clear he was jealous of Uzor. However, Selena was not a saint. She was terribly insecure, far worse than anyone Uzor had come across, and she enjoyed how far Uzor would go to prove his love for her. She flirts openly with different boys to incite Uzor's jealousy and if he did not react she would feel like she was losing him. She would tease Uzor, then feign her disinterest in him. Uzor couldn't talk to any other girl or her insecurities would spike and she would make sure Uzor felt guilty.

Uzor felt he was on an emotional rollercoaster. However, he never addressed the issue.

She was the Queen of Ego-stroking telling Uzor how great he was. He loved it. She made sure she pleased Uzor with her deep erotic kisses and touches. Everyone but Uzor noticed how deeply infatuated he was, far more than his short relationship with Frida. Uzor was 'catching feelings' a term that was circling around at the time and he felt his relationship with God and the Church disappear from his life. He was living one day to the next. Selena sent screenshots of her messages with other men. Some of whom Uzor knew, so Uzor would message the guys, thus creating more drama in his life.

Uzor's school performance was declining greatly, but he didn't care. His whole life was beginning to revolve around Selena, which was just how she wanted it.

One day, when heading to the city centre, a message from Stephan pinged into his phone.

'See you, ya worst cunt. Next time you better run, ya fucking chicken,' messaged Stephan.

Uzor was completely dumbfounded by the message. '?????' he messaged. 'How what's up?'

'Don't get wide with me, I swear. Ah'm goonna punch fuck out you. Fuck off, bye,'
Stephan messaged back.

Uzor continued to message, Uzor trying to understand why Stephan was sending such hateful messages. Stephan had a girlfriend himself. Then like a lightning bolt it hit Uzor. The reason why Stephan was sending all these messages was because Stephan wanted Selena.

Uzor went back to before he began dating Selena and remembered that Stephan had spoken fondly of her and had hidden his anger regarding Uzor's recent popularity in the group, so he felt that this was the perfect moment to strike. Uzor's fingers raced across the bottom of his phone screen.

'Is this about Selena?' messaged Uzor.

'Shut the fuck up ,ya fucking ugly basterd. Better find someone to back you up,' Stephan replied.

The insults continued to the group chat through the night, instilling fear in Uzor. He began to insult Stephan, but was only shooting himself in the foot. All of Stephan's boys except Michael and Simon ganged up against Uzor. He felt that everyone was against him because of Selena and became scared to enter the city centre or anywhere dense with people in Glasgow, only leaving when Michael and Simon were there to back him up. One evening, Stephan tried to square up to Uzor, but Michael and Simon stood between them and tried to talk sense into Stephan as he shouted Uzor's name. Uzor stood back afraid to fight Stephan. Stephan was now known for being crazy and carrying a knife at times. The C-Boys had greatly influenced Stephan and he had turned into more and more of a criminal.

Michael and Simon were successful at subduing Stephan, who treated the whole situation as some sort of joke, but he showed his hidden sadism that evening. After that situation Uzor started to avoid the city centre.

Arguments would sparked off in the groupchat with Uzor. Jasser was vehement and open about his dislike of Uzor, even wanting to fight him, his hate of Uzor coming from his popularity in the group, as Uzor seemed to attract the most women and was starting to gain influence over many of the members. Jasser wanted to assert his dominance as he was the original leader. One group member said, 'If Jasser or Uzor leaves the group it will fall apart.'

Uzor was kicked out of the groupchat many times then added back. At the same time Uzor and Selena would break up and make up multiple times. One day Uzor begged Selena for half an hour to take him back. The group was starting to fall apart. Uzor started to avoid it and spent more time focusing on the girls in his school year.

Bonfire Night was approaching and Uzor planned to meet up with four of the most popular girls in his year. Uzor and Fela were getting closer again. Fela didn't dislike him, unlike the rest of the group and they were spending more time with each other, along with Simon. The three planned to go to Bonfire Night to meet the girls. However before Uzor left, a voice stirred within him telling him not to go out. Uzor listened to the voice at first and decided not to go, afraid of meeting the group. But Uzor did not want to feel weak and he really wanted to go out, so he ignored the voice and the ominous feeling and left to meet Fela at his house, then Simon drove them to the city centre, parked and they walked to Glasgow Green.

Many were out that night and Uzor felt good, although his eyes were constantly on the lookout for any member of the group. Uzor messaged the girls and they met at the amusement rides set up on Glasgow Green. Uzor introduced his friends and they went together to the designated to check out the fireworks. After a long silence, the fireworks roared through the dark sky illuminating it. It was Uzor's first time at the Glasgow Green fireworks and the neon sprinkles of light sharpened all his senses. It was the most beautiful thing he had ever seen. His eyes were glued to them. The concentrated dust of light did not last long, but that short moment was enough to lift any-one's spirits and remove all thoughts of the group from Uzor's mind. They then all made their way out of the park. The girls made their way home and Uzor, Fela and Simon made their way to the Four Corners. The thought of the group quickly resurfaced and Uzor tried to per-suade his friends not to go to KFC, but they didn't listen.

'It will be fine. You won't see them,' said Simon.

They walked into KFC and ordered their food. Uzor felt safe. Maybe the voice he'd heard was just his own fears. Upstairs at KFC he looked outside at Jamaica and Renfield Street, which were packed with various people that were leaving Glasgow Green. The array of traffic lit up the roads. Uzor, Fela, and Simon left KFC and made their way to the carpark to go home when Uzor clocked the group walking down Argyle Street from the Bank of Scot-land. Uzor felt their presence and sped up.

'Let's go, man,' said Uzor

'It's cool, man. They won't touch you,' said Simon.

The closer the group got to him, the more uncomfortable he became. Uzor stood still, his adrenaline racing and tried to not look their way. Simon approached to dap one of the boys up when Uzor felt someone hit his ribs and head hard. The pain didn't register until a couple seconds later. Scream were uttered

'Here's stop that, my pal!' shouted one of the girls, who went to Uzor's secondary school.

Simon tried to ease the tension and started pushing them back, telling them that anyone who wanted to touch Uzor could sort it out with him. Simon led Uzor to his car a mile away from the Four Corners but the group, who had now found their prey, followed them. Uzor's whole mind was focused on getting home. He knew how fast the situation could deteriorate. They stopped at the turning at Howard Street. Michael was now influenced by the group screaming at Uzor, urging him for a square go. Michael's eyes bounced around and Uzor knew that he was under the influence of drugs. Suddenly, Stephan jumped in front of Michael warning him not to get too close to Uzor. Uzor was surprised. It was as if Stephan was backing him up. Simon again tries to subdue the tension and leads Uzor to his car. The group followed Uzor down Howard Street, and threw insults at him on Dixon Street all the way to the St Portland suspension bridge over the River Clyde.

Michael walked in front of them and after an exchange of words threw a hard hook at Uzor's cheekbones. All the built-up anxious rage spilled out of Uzor and he threw rapid hooks and jabs at Michael's face. They grabbed each other and threw punches at each other's faces. Uzor tucked in his head and closed his eyes to avoid seeing the punches. During this, several other boys began throwing punches at Uzor. Uzor was now being jumped. Uzor held his own, not falling once, but didn't know what to think. No thoughts ran through his head during the fight. He was blinded by rage and his instincts completely took over. Suddenly the fight was split up by Simon and Juilius. Uzor looked up to see Fela who gave Uzor a distant look: 'I don't want to be involved' was written all over his face. Simon, now angered, squared up to the group but after nobody squared up to him, he again led Uzor to his car. Stephan swaggered jokingly towards Uzor with a pocket knife but was stopped by one of the girls who screamed Stephan's name.

Uzor was still enraged and not thinking straight. He had never experienced anything like this before. Several boys, including Jasser and Alberto, followed Uzor past the bridge and tried to intimidate Uzor, calling him a 'bitch'. Uzor offered them a square go. However, after seeing Uzor's resolve in his eyes, he made it clear to the boys that he was no 'bitch'.

'Leave it, bro,' said Alberto's friend.

They left Uzor and headed back towards the bridge.

Simon, Fela and Uzor walk into the car park and get in, where Uzor begins joking about the event as a coping mechanism. He wanted to prove that he was fine. Fela and Simon started laughing unaware of Uzor's feelings about this traumatic event. They reached Uzor's house and he thanked Simon profusely for the lift, then walked up the stairs, opened the front door and entered his room. His parents were fast asleep.

It was at this point that Uzor began to get several calls from different people curious about Uzor's well-being. He kept his emotions to himself and acted like everything was fine. Then he called Selena.

'What happened?'she asked in concern.

It was at this point that Uzor's could not contain his emotions any longer and he burst into rage, sadness, despair and confusion, raining curses down on the group. tried to console Uzor but she was secretly holding in her joy over Uzor's unhappiness. To her, Uzor's misfortune was well deserved.

That night Uzor struggled to sleep. His mind raced back and forth. Hundreds of images of the event flashed through his mind, most importantly, those of Fela, his childhood friend, not backing him up saddened him deeply. All he felt was rage and resentment. The next day he continued cursing the group in front of his parents. His parents rebuked him: 'Why would you say that?' said his father

Uzor ran to his room.

No one seemed to understand the pain he was going through. They didn't seem to understand that he could have died on the bridge.

Chapter 23

Reflection

The next day at school, word spread on social media that Uzor had been jumped by the group. Many of Uzor's classmates, and those in different years, asked Uzor what had happened. Uzor was surprised.

'How do they know?' he wondered.

'Everybody knows, Uzor,' said one of the third-year boys.

Connie, who was known for his dislike of Uzor, even began defending him. The respect for Uzor from his schoolmates had skyrocketed overnight. Word spread that Uzor was making fun of the fight. The boys from the group were embarrassed and provoked Uzor.

'We're coming down to your area!' messaged Michael.

'Come down then. The boys are waiting for you,' messaged Uzor.

When Uzor mentioned that the hooligans in his neighbourhood, which included Louis and Junior, were backing him up, the group of boys made excuses as to why they could not come.

Uzor was not going down without a fight. For the rest of the time, Uzor did not leave his house for the city centre or other areas of Glasgow, as he was afraid to meet them. This time it would be permanent.

He continued to talk to Selena but started to have his doubts about her when she began to defend Michael and Jasser, and even hung around with them. It was at this point when walking up the hill to school that a voice rang in Uzor's ear – the same voice when he wanted to go out to Glasgow Green. This time, it prompted him to leave Selena. He knew Selena was toxic for him but because of all the adversity that he'd had to face, he couldn't help but feel regret for all the wasted time and energy. His stubbornness caused him to ignore the voice again. However, when walking up the hill again to school, the voice and feeling came back twice as strong, so Uzor took this as a strong sign: if he did not obey this voice something bad would soon occur.

So, on that hill, there and there, he took out his phone and with a huge amount of courage, he broke up with Selena. Instantly, a huge amount of weight lifted off Uzor's shoulders. He felt brand new. Throughout the day, Selena messaged hysterically and called Uzor for him to take her back. The roles had reversed and Selena did not like that. But Uzor had made up his mind. He was tired of the drama.

Months went by and with no girl in his life, Uzor used the girls in his school year to validate him.

A party was coming up and after promising the girls he'd take them to one of the parties he was invited to, he tried to get an invite. The guy holding the party didn't want Uzor there but after seeing that Uzor would be bringing girls he allowed him to come. On the party day Uzor took the girls to the party but the party organizers didn't allow him to stay once the girls had arrived. Instead, they kicked him out and the girls didn't bother to say anything to keep Uzor there. In the corridor next to the lifts. Uzor could do nothing but laugh, but it was a painful laugh. The girls would soon get boyfriends and forget all about Uzor – Uzor was only for parties.

That summer another party came along, which ended with Uzor getting into an altercation with the police and spending a night in the cell. It was in this red, cold and isolated cell that Uzor felt he had hit rock bottom. Everything he had experienced till now had damaged him psychologically and all he could do was cry.

Suddenly, Uzor experienced the same feeling that had told him to avoid Stephan, to avoid the group, to not go out on Bonfire Night and to leave Selena. The same feeling convinced Uzor to make the fateful decision to leave his secondary school and neighbourhood and spend his final year of secondary school at a more prestigious school; a school where he could start again and really focus on what he wanted to do in his life.

He would leave Fela who continued to smoke heavy amounts of marijuana, and Simon who continued to hang around the group, and embark on a new journey of self-discovery, which would allow him to truly decide what he wanted and remove the drama from his life. Solitary and alone: In loneliness he would find who he was.

Chapter 24

Different Perspective

Uzor's father enrolled him at the secondary school and he received his new school tie. The school tie officially sealed the deal and he prepared for his first day of Sixth Year. He took a shower, washed his short dreadlocks, got dressed in his new school uniform and made his way down the road. The sun was still shining. As he walked down, he suddenly became surrounded by different students from different schools in the area. He kept his eyes forward but maintained a scowl on his face. His experience with the group had hardened him and changed his view towards people.

The area Uzor's school was located was the complete opposite to his former secondary school. It was clean and spacious, the houses were upper middle class, and the myriad of fresh-looking plants and trees blessed his lungs. Uzor made his way down large steps and through a small, industrialized forest before crossing the road to his new secondary school. Many students hung around outside the school, awaiting the bell before they made their way into the school's Assembly Hall.

Everyone looked at Uzor with the same look he had received when attending his former schools. However, by this time Uzor was thoroughly used to it and paid no attention. He wasn't there for them. He walked in but wasn't allowed right into the School Main Assembly Hall because of the safety doors that could only be opened by the ladies working in the office.

'Oh hi! You're Uzor, aren't you? I'll get you outside the door to your right,' said the lady. Uzor noticed her light green eyes, as she pressed the button to let him in.

Uzor was overwhelmed by the influx of students in their school blazers chatting away. The sound in there resembled the conversation before a concert commenced. He walked to the door and met the lady. She gave Uzor his timetable and explained how things worked and who he could see about for tutoring. He then met the head teacher who also showed him the ropes, and introduced him to several different teachers including the deputy head teacher. Throughout this time Uzor kept his scowl and reserved demeanour, because of his past experiences.

While at school Uzor kept mostly to himself. He attended classes, talked to different students, but never went past small talk. The sixth years had their own space and Uzor would briefly appear in the room and then make his way to class or home. Many of his classmates did not approach Uzor as they felt intimidated. They couldn't read him and mostly kept their meetings with him very brief.

What made Uzor happy at the school was his art class. Uzor excelled in art, but the class was just for fun and not taken too seriously. The same could not be said about his other classes.

'I'm going to have to put you down for National 5,' sai his Graphics teacher

Uzor struggled academically but that hadn't dawned o him until now. He hadn't thought deeply about this problem at his former secondary school because he was distract ed by trying to fit in, by his poor decisions, his toxic friends and the chaos of his neighbourhood. However, he then go the worst mark in the English class at his new school – 6 per cent . When his English teacher read out his mark in front of the whole class, he was ashamed. One of the girls who sat opposite him on the class table smirked at him. He swallowed his emotions and left school early that day. He crossed the road, made his way through the thick forest pathway and up the stairs towards the long street home. It was there that he pulled out his phone from his pockets, paused the music playing on his earphones and called his dad. He then burst into tears

'Why do I keep failing? I got the lowest mark in the class!' cried Uzor.

His father consoled his son. Uzor had not been consoled like this since he was in primary school and felt defeated, as the stress of moving to a new school and being so alone was unleashed in that moment. All he could do was to go home and sleep.

The next day when Uzor walked home during his free period, he received a phone call from an organization who gave him a space to attend a charity week at Loch Eil. At first Uzor was going to deny the invitation but after hearing that he was a last-minute pick he couldn't say no. Uzor took the offer.

'I'll be going away for a week to Loch Eil,' said Uzor to his art teacher

'Nice. Enjoy, but make sure you are prepared to catch up,' he said.

After a few meetings with the organizers, he found himself on his way on the ferry bus to Loch Eil. While there at the camp, kayaking and playing multiple games, Uzor could only think about heading home. He got into arguments with many of the staff and did not really work well with the other team members, but his perspective on the trip changed when they made their way up the mountains at Loch Eil. He had to go up with his team members and they had to work together to go up the mountain. The destination was not clear to them. They carried heavy camping bags on their back, and walked and climbed for several hours with short breaks. It was mentally challenging and tedious, but Uzor felt liberated. At the highest point of the mountain his eyes gazed across the panoramic view. The fresh whistling air, the repetitive chug of the train down the mountain, the blue shimmering waters streaming into the lakes and the white-grey clouds revitalized him.

Though he was exhausted and wanted to reach the destination as quickly as possible he did not take the experience for granted. They finally reached their destination and began pitching their tents. Uzor looked at the beach half a mile away from him, the foreground covered by grass, and felt as if he was ascending to heaven as the sun shaped a diamond angel in the clouds. The white sandy beach and the slow cascading sea was captured in his memory . Pictures could not do it justice.

It was time to leave Loch Eil but the experience had impacted Uzor's perspective tremendously. Uzor fell asleep on the bus journey home, exhausted but healed by his serendipitous trip. He couldn't help but feel that God was looking out for him.

Uzor went back to school to be hit with the news from his art teacher that he was failing the course and that he would have to complete four pieces of art within a week. The frantic way in which his art teacher described his predicament instilled a sense of urgency in Uzor. His art teacher looked at him with a look of disapproval, but it wasn't a look of underestimation. In his teacher's eyes, Uzor sensed that he genuinely cared for his students' progress. The trip to Loch Eil had greatly changed Uzor and he felt a fire light up within him. His ambition, the ambition that he couldn't find anywhere else, the eternal flame within him, had been ignited and he was ready to pour himself into accomplishing something that he could be proud of.

He dropped his English class despite his teacher silently begging him not to and his Graphics class. The deputy head tried to dissuade him from dropping his classes, but Uzor had made his mind up.

He focused all his time and energy on art, bought special art pencils and markers and spent hours, days and weeks drawing and sketching, with his sole purpose to get an A that year. His art teacher encouraged him, putting Uzor through tests and challenges to check if he'd been studying. His teacher's way of teaching also inspired Uzor: he would stand on tables and mention an artist Uzor had heard of or not. Uzor's childhood love of art came back. His final challenge was to draw an A2-sized piece of art. His art teacher presented this challenge, and he took it.

At first, Uzor wanted to draw an A1-sized artwork but his art teacher, knowing Uzor thoroughly, knew that A2 would suit him better. Despite not drawing anything of that size before, Uzor attacked the task with an intensity that surpassed anything he'd attempted as a child. He spent hours deeply absorbed in the drawing as it came to life before him. He made sure he drew everything as exactly as it looked in real life, even staying up late at night to finish the artwork. As the deadline approached, Uzor stayed up late, only sleeping for one hour before heading to class to hand in his artwork. He was exhausted, but he couldn't help but feel immensely satisfied with himself. His father assisted him in attending art classes on the Tramway at the weekends.

He got deeply involved in the classes, even bringing in some of his art from there to improve his school portfolio.

At this time Uzor had completely separated from his former social life and spent more time working on himself. When his art teacher and head of department saw his A2 drawing in class they were speechless and held in their emotions as they praised Uzor's work.

'Thanks,' said Uzor nonchalantly

One of his classmates who sat next to him, a great artist in her own right, said, 'That's you guaranteed an A.'

Uzor was so focused on art that he spent less time in his other classes. His teachers began scolding him for it, even suggesting that he left. as he was in his last year, but Uzor held on, knowing the tremendous benefits to come. Uzor decided to attend university and follow his inclination to study art at university. He would forge his own path and was invited to some of the best universities in the UK. He noticed that he was the only African boy at all these unis, even the ones in London, which showed him how rare the direction he was taking was. He would use his loneliness as a catalyst to succeed.

The end of the school year approached and Uzor attended his prom. He didn't have any close friends or anyone to tell him who he should or should not be so he decided to express himself by wearing a tuxedo that earned him the title of 'Best dressed at Prom'. Even the teachers who disliked him complimented him that night.

Summer came and Uzor received his results through the mail. He quickly scanned to see his Art results. Sitting right in front of him was his A. Uzor was not very emotive, but his joy was reflected through his eyes.

So, this is what hard work does, he thought.

Uzor spent much of his summer on his own creating artworks and expressing who he truly was. He felt complete for the first time. He could buy what he wanted without the fear of being ridiculed and his love for himself started to truly develop. However, this was just the beginning. His next test would soon start at university where he would experience what it truly meant to be an African in Scotland.

Chapter 25

African Experience

The week just before freshers week at university, Uzor attended an African party with his mother. It was his mother's friends' children's party. It had been a while since he had attended an African party and he was looking forward to it. He was open to any bit of fun that summer. Uzor got on the bus to Bellahouston Park where the party was taking place in a youth hall. His outfit for the event wasn't something you would normally see in Glasgow, even in an urban area like the West End. He decided he would paint on his denim jacket and jeans and wear them to the African party, still expressing himself.

Before the party started, he helped set up the drinks and food tables and also got to know the DJ who played his favourite song. The party started at 3 p.m. but people made their way to the party at 5–6 p.m. and by 6 p.m. it was packed. Uzor got several looks from different people at the African party, but he didn't care. He was there to have a good time. A couple of his African friends from his church arrived including Fela.

Uzor and Fela had not seen each other in a while and their reunion was awkward, but as they talked, they got comfortable with each other. They sat at the table next to Uzor's father to continue their talk.

'How you getting on?' said Uzor, getting comfortable in his seat

'Been chilling with cousins and that. How about you?' said Fela, sipping his can of African Guinness Malt.

'I got into art school. How's Uni getting on for you?' said Uzor.

Fela's face immediately dropped. but he lifted it up to hide his true feelings. 'Not really enjoying it, but I just have to get on with it,' he said. Uzor wanted to give his friend some advice but he held himself back. He knew that whatever he said to Fela always fell on deaf ears. He refrained from saying anything and kept the conversation moving in a different direction. Silence took hold of the conversation and Fela left the table. Instead of worrying about Fela, Uzor took time to observe the party. Though he had attended many African parties with his parents he had never truly experienced one. He looked around and marvelled at the different African cultures and their different attires. The women wore their Gele hats and traditional dresses. The men wore their Ankara tops and trousers with their Fila hats. The Congolese men wore bright green-and-yellow-jewelled tuxedos with the fancy designer shoes, while the children ran around the dance-floor and corridors in their mini Ankara attires.

There were always drinks and puff-puffs in the middle of the table. If you weren't attentive enough someone would come and swipe your snacks and drinks without you noticing. Sometimes they would ask, but whether you said 'yes' or 'no' didn't matter because they were already gone before you could answer.

The aroma of Jollof, Fried, Boiled Rice, Pounded Yam wrapped in green leaf, PLANTAIN, egusi soup and various sweet-smelling stews massaged Uzor's nostrils. The line for the food was gigantic. The children were allowed up first and then the adults. The servers all chatted amongst themselves while serving the food. If the African food wasn't served to you aggressively by an overweight lady, it wasn't good food.

'What do you want? Do you want this one?' said the lady in pidgin, attentively listening for Uzor's answer.

The line was never straight. There would be people on either side of you. Sometimes the lines would stretch out to the nearest table. They wouldn't mind though; this was just normal procedures. There was something about jollof rice at parties. Its taste was unrivalled. Uzor wiped his plate clean in minutes.

'Man's hungry,' said Fela, making everyone around them laugh.

After eating, the DJ played the most requested and popular African songs: Davido, Wizkid, Burna Boy, and if the DJ was really good, he would play Lagbaja.

The women were the best dancers, and the men would join in with their wives on the dance floor. There was always one uncle who would sit at the tables with his sunglasses and cane indoors. Although some saw them as ridiculous, Uzor saw those uncles as the cool cats. He didn't want to join in but soon enough Fela and his African friends from church joined the dance floor prompting him to go along with it. The dance floor soon looked like a Nollywood film. By the end of the night, the floor was a mess. Uzor helped clean up but he would not forget the African experience again.

Chapter 26

The Old-School Mindset

His mother had many bags to carry with her, so she opted to be picked up by her friend's husband who was a taxi driver. His uncle pulled up to the front of the venue and, before greeting Uzor, he gave him a look of disgust. Uzor, as observant as he was, quickly took notice of the look but paid no attention.

'Good evening, uncle,' he said.

'Aaa how are you?' said his uncle.

Uzor sat in the front of the car while his mother sat at the back. Women were usually not permitted to sit next to another man in the front of the car. Uzor had a strange relationship with his uncle. He was standoffish and had a look that made him feel as if his opinion was not important. His eyes were distant like he was always half-listening to whatever you said. Despite this, his uncle was a great conversationalist. Most Africans were great conversationalists.

'So, a you now starting Unaversity?' said his uncle as he steered.

'Yes, I'm going to art school,' said Uzor.

'Art school? Why Art school? Isn't that what a female should be doing? You should be doing business. Now I know why you wore that strange outfit,' said his uncle.

Those words hit Uzor hard, but instead of defending himself, he ignored what his uncle said and kept his replies short. His uncle tried to play it off by saying, 'Well, You can always find someone who knows business to assist you with art.'

But the damage had already been done. Africans in general have an incredibly old-fashioned view of professions that are not related to health or engineering as they didn't make much money in their native countries. Money was the sole driving force for many Africans because it gave them status and respect, which parallelled his experience in the rough neighbourhood. It seemed that people who did not have much were the most materialistic. That evening Uzor got out of the car and helped his mother take the heavy bags upstairs. He felt the pent-up rage he had held in the car ride home bubble to the surface. His mother was also angered at what his uncle had said. Uzor decided that he would succeed through his art no matter what and prove everyone wrong, even though he knew it would not be easy.

Chapter 27

Art School

University had started and Uzor started to make some friends. At art school people were very expressive. They wore their own types of clothes, usually from vintage shops, even though they came from upper-middle-class homes. However, this was all to hide their true desire for materialistic and expensive things. Wearing vintage clothing was a mask to fit in; some sort of save-the-world act that kept them from being ostracized. What Uzor noticed was that many of them were just conforming, the complete opposite to how outsiders viewed art school.

Though he tried to make friends, the more he spent time around them, the more he realized he was different from them. Most of them, not all of them, could not be bothered working hard for a good grade. They just showed up, got paid and left. Uzor was different. He genuinely wanted to succeed, and he poured his heart and soul into the class.

His classmates took notice and began throwing passive-aggressive insults, especially after Uzor refused to go to clubs and parties with them.

One day their true feelings came out and they ganged up on Uzor. Seeing this as a recurrent theme in his life, Uzor stepped away from them and reverted to being alone, using his loneliness to spur him to accomplish something great. But it did not stop there. Some of his lecturers were not very fond of Uzor's tenacity and belittled him to the point that other students began to take notice. It was as if they wanted him to quit.

One of his classmates said, 'Just leave, Uzor!'

However, Uzor stuck to his guns. He hadn't come there to make friends; he didn't quit when things got hard. He knew how hard he'd worked to get into university, so he applied even more pressure on himself to win. Everything was stacked against him. People in his class were more skilled than him and he had to work twice as hard to get recognition, especially since he was the only African in the class. However, being the only African in the class did not deter him. He did not feel excluded. After all, he was used to being the only African and he had now come to accept it. He started creating more artworks outside of class and getting involved with other ambitious art-school students.

Chapter 28

The Scottish Experience

One of the ambitious art school students was a Japanese photographer called Junya, who took an interest in Uzor's artwork and invited him on a photography trip in Scotland. Uzor saw this as a chance for him to improve his university portfolio and find inspiration for his artwork. Uzor accepted and that same week they were on their way up the M8. As Junya drove up the motorway, feelings from the time Uzor had been a passenger driving on the motorway during his childhood came flooding into his mind. Uzor looked out to see the speeding cars racing by him and the beautiful landscape of Glasgow as he passed by the River Clyde. He noticed that Glasgow had a lack of skyscrapers, which is probably why no one ever looked up because the architecture was within view. The weather was mild: it drizzled a bit, but the rain wasn't cold, as it battered the front and back windscreens.

Soon they crossed the Erskine bridge. He looked out to see the miniature buildings down below. They passed Loch Lomond and Junya pointed out a beautiful loch, animated by shimmers of light that looked like butterflies filled with beams of light. The view was heavenly. Uzor pulled out his camera to take a picture, but the effect was not the same. They finally ended up in Glen Coe. The vast mountains with their hazel gardens and faraway mountains with their snow-covered peaks excited Uzor. He could not take his eyes off them. The road they were on seemed to stretch to infinity. Uzor took everything in like a child, absorbing every minute detail. As they went further along the path Uzor looked to his left and immediately felt a strange connection to a house that stood alone in the middle of the vast, otherworldly space. The house stood proudly, despite not fitting in. It looked close, but was several miles away. The house seemed to be calling to him. Junya stopped to take pictures and Uzor walked on to look at the house. The more he looked at the house and looked around the terrain, the more his love for Scotland grew.

'Wow'! was the only thing Uzor could repeat in his mind.

On the way home Uzor began to reflect on his experience in his rough neighbourhood and began to develop a love for it. He laughed at certain events that had taken place and at the fact he had tried to become Scottish by completely disregarding his African identity.

It was in Junya's car that he made the decision to combine both sides of his life. He saw that running away from either side was the reason he had experienced so much pain. He had tried to run away from his identity but if he had only listened, he would have found out earlier that he was not African or Scottish – he was an AfroScot.

AfroScot, he thought Uzor

The term came to him in a flash, but he would keep the idea dormant in his mind. The more he thought of it the more liberated he felt and the more open he became.

The journey back was filled with laughter and banter Junya dropped him off on Princes Street, in Edinburgh.

'Thank you! Enjoy your weekend in Edinburgh' said Uzor as Junya headed off.

Uzor walked down Princes Street and stopped at a bus stop near Waverley Station to observe the different kinds of people that walked down the street.

They are all different, he thought .

Uzor contemplated the fact that many people tried to change who they were and be someone else but if they just looked around, they would notice that nobody looked like, or had the same experiences as, them. That is something no one could take away from anyone. That is what made people unique and exceedingly rare individuals.

Uzor left the bus stop to get the next train to Glasgow from Waverley Station. However, due to his tiredness he read the train schedule incorrectly, and got on the wrong train.

When he got on the train, he was fully aware the train was going a completely different way but decided to test it with the conductor. She came around and looked at his ticket to Glasgow, but didn't refuse his ticket and continued walking down the train.

I'm probably just thinking too much, Uzor thought.

Uzor relaxed on the train and began reading a book when his attention was soon pulled away to the train window. The train was speeding by a vast sea; the bluest sea he had ever seen. He pressed his eyes to the window and looked down to see a large rock with a house on it, on its own separate island. Uzor looked to the opposite train window to see the blue clear sea stretching to the end of the world. The scene intrigued Uzor. The thought of being on the wrong train resurfaced but he quietened it down. He took out his phone once again to take photos, but it wasn't the same as what he saw.

Where am I? he wondered.

He took out his phone and turned on his location to locate where he was on Google Maps.

The further the train went, the more the view resembled a wonderland. The houses were painted in different colours like the buildings in Blackpool. Behind the buildings were beaches. The wild racket of the train could not disturb the serene peace Uzor was experiencing. Soon the train began to empty, and he reached the final stop.

'Excuse me. Does this train go back to Edinburgh?' asked Uzor.

'No!' said the conductor.

Uzor by now had accepted the situation even though he was surprised to discover that it would take another two hours to get back to Glasgow. He went to the other side of the train station to catch the incoming train back to Edinburgh Waverley.

'Where are you going?' asked the train conductor.

'Edinburgh Waverley,' said Uzor

'No train goes that way. This train goes to Edinburgh' said the train conductor with a serious face.

Uzor, now confused, went back to the other side, aboard the train. When Uzor asked the ticket inspector why she had told him 'no' when he asked if the train goes to Edinburgh, she simply replied, 'I don't know why I said that. Been a long day'

Now it was too dark to witness the wonders of the ride back but Uzor implanted this memory of Scotland deep in the crevices of his memory. He got off the train at Edinburgh and then caught the right train to Glasgow Queen Street.

Chapter 29

The Afro-Scot Experience

Uzor left Queen Street and walked down Buchanan Street towards St Enoch's, where heIt
was at St Enoch that Uzor crossed paths with
Simon. Simon looked at him with surprised eyes
and hugged Uzor.

'Bro, long time! How have you been? I have
been seeing your artworks! Maaad, bro,' he said .

'For real, bro? I have been good! How about
you?' said Uzor.
Simon began telling Uzor all the crazy things that
had gone on since Uzor had left the group.

'Some of the C-Boys are in prison and some
dons have criminal records and shit. I even got
involved, bro. The group's no more g. It's been
mad!' said Simon.

Where was I when all this was happening?
wondered Uzor.

Though the meeting was brief, Uzor knew
there and then that he had made the best decision to leave the group.

Uzor and Simon said their goodbyes and Uzor got on the bus home. He went upstairs, took his seat and began reading the same book he had been reading on the train to Glasgow when Fela also came upstairs and sat beside him. Uzor closed his book and began making small talk. However, this time Fela began opening up.

'Bro! I have been seeing what you have been doing and I am inspired, man. I failed my biomedical studies at university and my parents are not too happy. It is a bit peak, but after seeing you I want to go and study music. Even if I fail, at least I can say I did it,' said Fela.

Fela's confession made a lasting impression on Uzor. For years, Fela had been afraid of blazing his own trail and becoming the person he wanted to be. He was so oppressed by his parents and everyone around him that he had turned to drugs and alcohol to soothe his pain, but now he had finally made up his mind. The look in Fela's eyes made it clear that he was determined to follow through with his plans.

Several months passed and Uzor met Fela again on the bus but this time Fela was beaming with confidence. He could not hide his joy. He was full of purpose. They began talking about Fela's course and Uzor listened attentively, knowing how important music was to him. Fela began sharing music by Fela Kuti and various old-school jazz musicians that intrigued Uzor. Fela also began quitting his habit of smoking.

'My parents decided to give me the chance. If I can stick it to the end and make something of myself, they said they will continue to support me.'

Fela's joy and excitement inspired Uzor. For years they had both tried to fit into being somebody they were not, trying to fit into Scotland and behaving like they were something they were not. But now through solitude and introspection they had identified the true cause of their pain. It was their lack of identity.

By finding that they were not just Africans or Scottish, but AfroScots, it allowed them to walk with confidence and accept their role in life. Suddenly, the memory of the 'AfroScot' came back to Uzor. Through the help of the Glasgow Art Community and the African Community Uzor decided to open an ART GALLERY called 'The AfroScot Experience', to document his experience of being an African in Scotland, so that young kids and people struggling with their identities would understand that they aren't the only ones and they would come out better.

On the opening day of the gallery many turned up following the dress code, wearing African attire and mixing it with their Scottish attires. The food choice was a mix of both African and Scottish food. It was fun seeing JOLLOF RICE eaten with haggis and seeing Scottish kids tuck into pounded yam and drinking malt.

Uzor finally felt complete.

He did not need to be Scottish and speak with a Glasgwegian accent and he did not need to find his 'African Brothers'. All that was right within him.

Your direction in life does not have to be a roller-coaster. Sometimes, it can be a slow drag through the desert where your destination is the sweet-water-filled watermelon in the middle of the sea of sand.

Keep moving forward and remember God is always in the details.

The Afro-Scot Experience

NOTES

NOTES

NOTES

NOTES

NOTES